101 BIG IDEAS
FOR PROMOTING
A BUSINESS ON A
SMALL BUDGET

Barbara Lambesis

Marketing Methods Press
Phoenix, Arizona

Printed in the United States of America.

I dedicate this book to William E. Molloy, an unequaled spirit of tireless support and patience and a remarkable entrepreneur, and to Chris and Niko Lambesis, my wonderful sons who have never tried to discourage me from expending the effort it has taken to succeed at the various ventures I have attempted.

Acknowledgments

Many small business owners encouraged me to expand my original booklet of the same title into a paperback handbook. Were it not for them, I would never have set aside the time to do it. Their "demand" for the information contained in this publication literally forced me into developing this "product" and getting it into the marketplace. Not only did they encourage me to become an author, they also have been a great source of personal inspiration. While working with hundreds of small business owners, I was constantly amazed and delighted by the ingenious spirit of today's entrepreneurs. Their enthusiasm has been so genuine and contagious. Their dreams so vivid and compelling. While they are forced to do so much with so little, and often face enormous barriers to their success, their resourcefulness and energy never abates. Because their heroic efforts are rarely rewarded with wealth, they often must settle for simpler satisfaction. For example, I remember the excitement of a client who called me to say she had finally made a real and meaningful contribution to society. She had hired her first employee and provided someone with a job and a livelihood. Well, that's not so insignificant if you ask me. So, I am grateful to the many small business owners who provided the encouragement and inspiration to write this book. I hope it will serve as a useful tool to help them and their colleagues reach their business goals and realize their dreams.

Small business owners are not the only ones I wish to acknowledge. When associates and friends learned of my undertaking, many offered several of the "big ideas" contained herein and made useful suggestions to improve the content. Those generous contributions will always be appreciated. In addition, Randy Weiss, Bill Molloy and Steve Hutchison provided proof reading and editing services. Jenny Reilly retyped the manuscript umpteen times without complaint and also assisted with the production of the book. Cindy Mackey was responsible for the terrific cover design. Thanks to you all! I am grateful for your help and support.

TABLE OF CONTENTS

Chapter 3 - Personal Sales 53

Chapter 4 - Public Relations & Publicity 63

Chapter 5 - Sales Incentives 75

Chapter 6 - Organizing Your Activities . . 85

INTRODUCTION

Promoting Your Business

If you are like most small business owners, you are probably very uncomfortable with the whole idea of promoting your business. Don't worry, you are not alone. Frankly, most business owners feel much better about their ability to produce the goods and services, manage the employees, watch the cash flow and deliver the customer service, than they do about their ability to reach and motivate new customers through promotional activities.

Small business owners often feel at a loss when it comes to business promotion. They realize that great sums of money can be wasted on efforts that produce little or no results. They seldom feel confident about selecting the right activities for their business. Some are so paralyzed by the fear they may lose money on promotional activities that they do little or nothing at all to promote their business. Others think only very creative people have the talent to be good at business promotion or that it takes lots of money to have an effective program. Some think promotion can only be done right by marketing professionals, whose fees are beyond their reach.

This handbook should help to dispel many of these notions, as well as stress the importance of business promotion to the success of any company. Promotional activities play a key role in a company's marketing strategy. If you have carefully selected your target market, identified its needs, developed a product or service to meet the needs, found ways to make it easy for your potential customers to get what you have to offer and priced your offering so your prospects can afford it, you are ready for business success. WHAT'S MISSING? The key ingredient, promotion. If you don't let potential customers know about your goods or services, you will never make a sale.

When a company makes its potential customers or clients aware of the benefits they will receive from its products - the goods or services it offers - it's actively promoting the business. How a company goes about promoting itself will have a tremendous impact on the identity and image the business has in the marketplace.

Seasoned business owners know that no single method of promotion will be enough to reach and motivate the vast majority of potential customers in their market territories. Therefore, the smart business owner will select 10 -12 promotional activities to use on a consistent basis. The key to successful promotion on a small budget is *consistency* over a long period of time. A business must be consistent in the methods it uses to promote the business and the messages it sends to attract the customers. That means successful business promotion requires a strong commitment to a realistic plan that invests adequate resources of time and money.

Promotional activities generally fall into one of five major categories:

Advertising
Packaging
Personal Sales
Public Relations/Publicity
Sales Incentives

In this handbook, each category is explained and 101 different promotional methods are described. To help you develop a plan for promoting your business, follow these simple steps:

First, read through each of the various promotional methods and put a check in the brackets at the bottom of those methods you think might work for your business.

Next, give more thought to each activity you checked and determine what your budget can afford and if your preferred customers will be reached and motivated by the methods you are considering.

Finally, select the best 10 -12 methods and complete the chart at the end of the handbook. The chart will help you organize your promotional strategy over a one-year period.

Promoting your business can be both creative and fun, especially when ingenuity and resourcefulness are employed. The ideas in this handbook are tried and true methods used by thousands of successful small business owners. Many of the ideas should work for your business, too.

We're always looking for more "Big Ideas." So, if you have a promotional idea you'd like to share with others, send it to us. We'll even pay you $10 if we use your idea in the future. Just complete the handy form in the back of the handbook and maybe you'll see your "Big Idea" and your name in our next publication.

CHAPTER ONE

ADVERTISING

What's advertising? Advertising is the **PAID** placement of a message or messages to promote the goods or services of a business. The company placing the advertising has complete control over the message used and the delivery system. The control is possible because the owner of the company is paying for the activity. Any time you pay to have a message delivered to your customers or potential customers, you are advertising.

Unfortunately, many small business owners waste their limited resources by not being careful about where, when or how they advertise.

Since it is unlikely that small business owners will have the means to purchase large quantities of radio and TV air time, print advertising space and billboards, you may need to select more personal and direct methods to advertise your business. Here are some simple tips to help you get the most out of your advertising efforts and your advertising dollars.

First, control your destiny. Don't become the prey of every advertising salesperson that comes along. With a simple and solid marketing strategy and promotion plan you won't become a victim of haphazard advertising. Haphazard advertising usually occurs when sales are slow and the business owner starts to panic. Suddenly, in walks an advertising salesperson with a "special" that can't be refused. The depressed business owner falls for the sales pitch, without really considering whether or not the advertising vehicle is right for the business. Moreover, the sales representative usually "helps" the business owner create an ad right on the spot. Little planning or thought goes into the development of the ad. With this approach to advertising, the commissioned advertising salesperson is in control, not the business owner. As a result, the advertising usually produces few sales, if any, and the business owner complains that he/she tried advertising once and it just didn't work.

To avoid these occurrences, take charge of your advertising and promotion plan. If you plan your advertising and promotional activities, selecting those that are likely to reach and motivate your potential customers, you can let advertising sales representatives know that their offer just doesn't fit in with your marketing strategy. Most importantly, you will avoid spending your cash on advertising that doesn't work.

Second, choose your approach. Decide what you will emphasize in your advertising. Your approach should be one that you believe in and with which you are comfortable. If you don't believe in what you are presenting to the public, nobody else will.

To select your approach, remember the needs and wants of your preferred customer. Do they seek your goods or services because they are convenient, economical or high quality? Do they associate status or belonging, health or well-being, approval or self-esteem

6

with your offering? Do they come to your business because the service is friendly?

Examine your entire business, including the environment, service capability, facilities, dress of employees, and attitude toward the customer. Determine what you think makes your business different from your competition. Decide what you think is your biggest plus and see if your current customers agree. If so, that characteristic should be the thrust of your advertising approach. See if you can create an advertising slogan by describing your greatest business asset in ten words or less.

Some well known and effective advertising slogans are:

> **"You're in Good Hands with Allstate."** (Allstate Insurance)
> **"Tastes Great, Less Filling."** (Miller Lite Beer)
> **"Ace is the place with the helpful hardware man."** (Ace Hardware)
> **"Good Times, Great Taste at McDonald's."** (McDonald's Restaurants)

Use your slogan, even if it is in small print, on all your advertising. Some marketing minded business owners print their slogan on business cards and company stationery as well.

Third, select the media. To be effective, you must select more than one method to advertise your business. No single vehicle will reach and motivate all your prospects and customers. While all advertising will have the same approach, choosing the right media will be important. Select several methods to promote your business. You can select the right methods for your business from the various activities that are described later in this handbook. Repeat your advertising in the selected media as often as you can afford to do so.

Fourth, develop an advertising and promotion budget. There are several ways to determine an appropriate budget. Some of the more common ways are to determine a percentage of the operating budget, an amount per unit, or a percentage of gross receipts to apply to advertising and promotion. Remember it is important to set aside some money, time and resources for marketing and advertising if you want your business to survive.

In the beginning, expect to spend about 15-20 percent or more of gross receipts on marketing and advertising. Depending on the type of business you operate, that figure should drop to about 5-10 percent once the customer base is firmly established.

Fifth, give your advertising and promotion plan time to work. A business owner should develop a plan that covers at least one full year. A simple way to organize a yearly plan is described at the end of this handbook. The owner must be willing to stick to the plan, making adjustments after six to eight months. With a small budget, it takes time for an advertising and promotion plan to show results. Be patient, there are no instant results. Think of your advertising and promotional activities as a snowball rolling down a hill, gaining size and momentum with each turn. You must give your plan time to work, if you want to gain the benefits of consistent advertising and promotion.

Finally, be consistent. It is important that all advertising be consistent in message, methods and image. Make a commitment to one particular advertising approach and stick to it. Choose appropriate advertising and promotion vehicles, add your slogan, implement your advertising and promotion activities on a regular basis and follow your plan.

There are several categories of advertising you can consider:
print advertising,
broadcast advertising,
sales tools,
reminder advertising and
attention getters.

The following describes some "Big Ideas" in each of these categories.

PRINT ADVERTISING

#1 Classified Ads

Classified ads can be run in daily and weekly newspapers, magazines and classified-ad newspapers. Sometimes, classified ads get better results than display ads and are much less expensive. They work best for personal services, home improvement services and many items that people often purchase used. Nevertheless, one look in the Sunday classified section of any metropolitan newspaper probably will convince you that almost anything can be sold through the classified section. Classified ads are not just for yard sales and used cars. Many special interest magazines also offer classified ad space. By selecting the right publications, the business owner can carefully target the ad to potential prospects. Classified advertising rates usually are based on the number of words, lines or inches in the ad. Read the classified sections of the papers and magazines you are considering to determine what category best fits your products or services. Then, copy a style that gets your attention and try to write your ad to make it stand out from the others in the same category. The classified section also is a place where you can test several messages for appeal before you use the message in more expensive display ads or printed materials. Develop several ads and pick the best two or three that you think will attract customers. Then rotate the ads in the same publication, or place the same ad in several publications to determine which evokes the better response. Some publications also offer display classifieds that should be considered as well. Don't try to save dollars by making your classified ad too short. Be sure to include enough facts to get attention and avoid using too many abbreviations. Run the ad several times in the publications you feel are read by your potential customers to adequately determine the effectiveness of this advertising vehicle.

[ ] This idea or its modification could work for my business.

#2 Co-op Advertising

Co-op advertising is advertising that shares its cost among several parties - usually the retailer, distributor and manufacturer. If you put the name of a product you sell in your ads, you may be able to negotiate with the manufacturer or supplier and get them to agree to share the cost of advertising with you. Sometimes, the supplier will be willing to split the cost fifty-fifty with the retailer. Ask for advertising support from the companies whose products and services you carry. Some newspapers even have a cooperative advertising department that assists a company in seeking ad money from suppliers. Cooperative advertising arrangements can go a long way to help the business owner get at least part of the advertising paid for by the supplier or manufacturer. For example, a grocery store may get most of its advertising paid for by the suppliers of products it features in weekly ads. The concept also has worked with ingredients like Scotchguard, Wool and Teflon. Every year millions of co-op dollars go unused. Small business owners should find out if they qualify for co-op advertising dollars and use them to lower their advertising expense.

[ ] This idea or its modification could work for my business.

#3 Customized Advertising Columns

There are a number of companies that produce and distribute personalized newspaper column advertising for many service professionals. A subscriber pays between $15-25 each week for a fresh column on a topic related to the subscriber's profession. The column carries the picture of the subscriber, useful information and a personal closing message. It looks like a newspaper column written by the subscriber. The subscriber buys advertising space in the local newspaper to run the column each week. Sometimes called advertorials, these columns are a softer sell than a display ad and can work well for realtors, health care professionals, accountants and attorneys. If you have the time and writing skills, you can write your own column and save the subscription fees. Always provide useful information that potential clients or customers really need. They will be grateful for the information and view the author as a credible authority who is genuinely interested in helping people solve their problems. Make sure the column carries a photo of the author.

[ ] This idea or its modification could work for my business.

#4 Magazine Advertising

Magazine ads tend to instill consumer confidence in the company or the product being advertised. Local magazines or regional editions of national magazines offer lower advertising rates. Also, you can run an ad once in a prestigious publication, have the ad reprinted, and use the reprint for several years as a flier. Because there are hundreds of specialty and trade magazines, magazine ads can be targeted directly to your audience, sending your message to the most likely prospects. Magazines have a longer shelf-life, so your ad may be viewed several times by the same reader. Also, because of the quality of the paper used in magazines, they are a better medium if you want to advertise in color. Have a magazine size ad ready to go at all times. Tell the advertising representatives of the magazines you wish to use that you are a small business on a very tight budget and are interested in buying only last-minute, unsold space at greatly reduced rates. You may need to wait several editions, but you will save enormous amounts of money. If you use a prestigious local or national magazine to advertise your products, mention this in your other advertising vehicles, "As seen in....magazine."

[ ] This idea or its modification could work for my business.

11

#5 Newspaper Ads

Always have your newspaper and print ads initially designed and produced by a capable graphic artist. No matter what the ad salesperson says, most newspaper ad departments are not able to produce effective display ads. Pay for the general design of a basic ad, with a window of space to insert information about your offers. Then, have it reproduced in several sizes or use it as a model for later ads produced by the paper. Also, good copy writing is essential to make your ad appealing and to make it stand out from the other ads. Be sure to run your ads on the right day and test the effectiveness of the various newspapers you have selected by doing a coupon advertisement or special offer. After you have given the newspapers a few months to test, drop the ones that do not draw. A good ad can be run over and over again; only you will become bored with it. On a small budget, it is unlikely you can run it often enough or large enough for complete saturation to occur. A good ad can last 2-3 years, especially if it is designed with a window to insert special offerings. Excellent ads also can be re-printed and used as statement stuffers, fliers, hand-outs, mailers or even enlarged and used as a poster.

[ ] This idea or its modification could work for my business.

#6 Newspaper Inserts

Newspaper inserts often work better than display ads. You can produce your own sales sheets, fliers or mini-catalogs and have them inserted and delivered with a local newspaper. Usually, the advertiser must deliver the pre-printed materials to the newspaper at least one week in advance of distribution. Also, contact in advance the local advertising representative of the newspaper for any special requirements. Most often, the publisher will charge a few pennies per insert to deliver it with the newspaper. Inserts are especially effective when delivered with smaller, community newspapers that don't regularly carry large quantities of inserts. An insert can really catch attention when it literally falls in the reader's lap. In addition, the interested reader can easily put the insert aside for future reference without having to cut up the newspaper. To test the effectiveness of this method, include a coupon, limited-time offer, or ask the customer to bring the insert to your place of business to register for a prize or receive a free gift or discount. Make sure the insert is eye catching and projects the appropriate image for your business.

[ ] This idea or its modification could work for my business.

#7 Per-Order / Per-Inquiry Ads

Some radio, TV, newspaper, and magazine ad departments will allow per-order or per-inquiry arrangements with local advertisers. With these arrangements, the company provides the ad, but does not pay for space or air time. Instead, the company pays the radio station, TV station, newspaper or magazine an amount agreed on in advance for every order or inquiry generated by the ad. The advantage of this arrangement is no up front costs to the advertiser. However, these arrangements are not easy to negotiate, since the deal must be attractive to the media to entice them to participate. The TV, radio station or publication must feel they can make money on the arrangement before they will get involved with per-order or per-inquiry advertising contracts. In addition, a mechanism must be set up so that orders and inquiries generated by the ad can be monitored. If you think you have a product or service that can be promoted through this method, and you are willing to share the profits, explore this possibility.

[ ] This idea or its modification could work for my business.

#8 Program and Yearbook Ads

Advertising in programs of local sporting and performing arts events and in high school yearbooks can be an effective and inexpensive way to promote your goods and services near schools or sports fields. This will be true only if you have products that are targeted to students, parents or sports fans. If you are placing an ad just to support your child's drama club, marching band or Little League team, consider it a donation or a public relations expense and don't expect any sales results. On the other hand, if your ad offers a coupon, sales incentive or donation to the appropriate organization with every purchase and you have products and services designed for these markets, you may be able to generate lots of sales for very little advertising expense. You also will generate some community good will.

[ ] This idea or its modification could work for my business.

#9 Yellow Pages

Before signing a contract with a commissioned Yellow Pages sales representative, determine if your business will generate sales by placing an ad in the Yellow Pages larger than the standard courtesy line. Ask the question, do most people looking for products or services such as yours consult the Yellow Pages to find them? Then call businesses similar to yours which are running display ads and ask the question, "I found you in the Yellow Pages, do most of your customers find you that way?" If the answer is "yes" and the Yellow Pages look promising, you can increase your response rate by carefully writing the ad copy and sizing your ad as large as your competitors. Experts suggest you give as much information about your offering as you can, without overcrowding the ad. Ads are billed monthly to your phone bill and begin only after the Yellow Pages are published and delivered. There are many variations to the Yellow Pages. Use caution before placing an ad in competing directories. Most are not very effective and all are expensive. The Yellow Pages are popular because they have a reputation for being an effective advertising medium. That reputation has been reinforced by the advertising the company does to promote its directory. Moreover, everyone has heard of the Yellow Pages. Some advertisers will get more results from their advertising dollar in the Yellow Pages than from any other advertising method. Even so, most business owners are dissatisfied with the results they get from the Yellow Pages. That's because the Yellow Pages advertising does not create a desire on the part of the potential customer to buy. The Yellow Pages simply direct the customer, who is ready to buy, to the seller. While Yellow Pages advertising can generate new customers and clients, increase sales and add to the bottom line, too often dollars spent with the Yellow Pages are not used wisely. To get the most from your Yellow Pages advertising dollar, don't depend on the Yellow Pages alone. You need to develop a cost-effective, total advertising and promotion plan to direct customers to your business. Then, when they are ready to buy, customers can easily find you in the Yellow Pages. However, never ask customers in your other advertising to look for you in the Yellow Pages. To do so simply courts disaster. When the prospect goes to the Yellow Pages to find you specifically, he will be confronted with all your competitors. He may decide to call or visit a competitor that is closer or to get price comparisons on the phone.

[ ] This idea or its modification could work for my business.

BROADCAST ADVERTISING

#10 Radio

Radio advertising gives the business owner a chance to reach customers or clients with a spoken or musical message. Unlike print advertising that requires the prospect to read the message, radio advertising takes no effort on the part of the listener. Another advantage of radio is its ability to reach a more selected target market than newspapers, because different stations in large markets appeal to different audiences. To determine if radio will work for you, ask your current customers if they listen to the radio. If they answer yes, then ask them what stations they listen to and when. Before exploring radio further, it's a good idea to establish a profile of your preferred customer. Identify the demographic characteristics of your customer base and match it to the demographics of a station's listeners. Insist that the radio advertising sales representative provide you with accurate information about the station's audience and size. The station ad representative can send you the information. Some stations will trade "air time" for products and services they can use with radio promotions. Most will routinely negotiate rates. If you want to identify your product with a special radio personality, give a sample of the product or service to the announcer and let him do an ad from an outline you have provided. Often you get more time than the 30 or 60 seconds allowed for a taped or scripted ad. If your budget is small, you'll get the most from your radio ads if you stagger them by running them two weeks on and one week off. Concentrate airing your ads during a few days of the week or only on the programs you know potential customers listen to. Also, if appropriate, explore co-op ads in which you mention the products of your suppliers and share the cost of the radio ads with them.

[ ] This idea or its modification could work for my business.

#11 Television

If you are not careful, you can spend a lot of money on television and get little in return. Television advertising is not a wise choice for most small business owners. Nevertheless, television commercials are effective if used properly, even by the "little guy." Television advertising cannot be used by the small business owner in the same way that beer companies or auto manufacturers use TV advertising. The small business owner simply doesn't have the budget to air a large number of commercial spots. As a general rule, don't bother with TV ads if you can't purchase enough to repeat your message to your customer base several times a week and maintain the TV ad campaign for three months. The exception to this rule is placing your commercial advertising on targeted programs. An owner of a local tackle and bait shop does very well by purchasing only one 30-second commercial each week on a local fishing show. Bargains also can be found on local cable and low frequency stations. The key to success in these cases is to carefully target the programs that will carry your commercial. Most commercial rates are open to negotiation, but remember you must add on the cost to produce the ad, as well as the cost of the air time, to establish your TV advertising budget. Again, look for co-op advertising opportunities. Some small business owners find it pays to work with a media placement agency to place their TV ads. Since the agencies buy air time in such large quantities, they frequently can negotiate lower rates which they pass on to their clients. In addition, their knowledge of the programming available through local stations can help you get your ads placed on the right programs. TV is a powerful medium and can work wonders; however, it must be used wisely or it can be a very expensive mistake.

[ ] This idea or its modification could work for my business.

18

SALES TOOLS

#12 Brochures & Pamphlets

Brochures offer a wonderful opportunity for a business to provide lots of details about the goods or services it offers. A brochure should give plenty of information about all aspects of the product. For example, it should explain the features and benefits offered, proof of the claims, the extent of any guarantees or warranties and how a potential customer can obtain the goods or services. Including testimonials from satisfied customers and, if appropriate, the credentials of the management staff can be effective in establishing the credibility of a company. Since brochures can be expensive to produce, the method of use and means of distribution should be established before production begins. Too many brochures end up in a box in the closet or in back of the store because their purpose as a sales tool was not carefully considered before production. Don't depend on a brochure to sell your product or service for you. A brochure should provide the potential customer with additional information required to make a decision. However, the information provided in the brochure or pamphlet is only one step in the sales and communication process. Have your brochures professionally produced. You can give the project to a public relations or advertising agency or act as your own producer and hire a writer, photographer (if required), graphic designer and printer. In either case, you can save money by being prepared. Prepare a detailed outline or draft copy of the information you want in the brochure. Gather all the source material, illustrations and photos you need in advance. Finally, provide the graphic designer with brochure samples representing design styles that appeal to you. Taking these steps will not only save you time and money, they also will help to produce a brochure or pamphlet with which you can be happy.

[ ] This idea or its modification could work for my business.

#13 Bulletin Board Signs

Place signs with tear-off coupons containing your business phone number on bulletin boards in grocery stores, community centers, banks, churches, etc. These signs work well for service businesses like housekeeping, baby-sitting, piano or computer lessons, lawn care, home improvement and auto repair. They also can work well for some products and personal care services such as hair cuts, manicures, massages, personal valet services and shopping or gift services.

[ ] This idea or its modification could work for my business.

#14 Business Cards

Your business card can be your most effective sales tool. Always have your business card with you. Let your business card serve as one of your best advertising tools by adding additional information to it. Along with the standard company name and logo, person's name, address and telephone number, add information about what products and services your company offers. In fact, have the card produced with a tab on top so your company name will stick out above the others when filed in the business card box or rolodex file. Additional information about your company can be printed on the back or inside of a double-sized, folded card. When you obtain cards from new business acquaintances, always write on the back the location or the event at which you met. Later, if you need to contact the person you can mention details of your meeting. The contact will be impressed with your interest in remembering him/her. If you think the individual is a good prospect for future sales, file the newly acquired card in a separate "prospect box" for future follow-up.

[ ] This idea or its modification could work for my business.

#15 Direct Mail

Direct mail advertising can allow a company to carefully target its market. With direct mail marketing, the recipient of the material can be taken right through the entire sales process. By including an order form, coupon or a toll-free number, a company can show what it has to offer and provide a means to make the sale. However, direct mail is very costly and can be ineffective. Careful planning, testing and a good mailing list are critical to the success of this method. When developing a direct mail piece, gather a collection of direct mail advertising you receive at your home or business. Sort through and save the ones that appeal to you. Then show a few to some of your best customers and ask which they most likely would respond to. Test a few approaches with a limited mailing in advance to see the response rate, then choose the strongest package and send out your mass mailing. Expect a one to two percent return at most. If you cannot make money with a one or two percent response, don't try direct mail. Also, it often takes two or three repeat mailings to get a prospect to buy. Direct mail works best for mail order products, but can be used to announce store openings, sales, free seminars and professional services available in the neighborhood. You can get pre-printed mailing labels from many local and national mailing list companies that can be located in the Yellow Pages. The right mailing list is paramount to success. It is important to get the most up-to-date list for your mailing, so ask the producer when the data for the list was collected and if it is updated on a regular basis. Mailing list companies all charge about the same, but some lists are much better than others. Some companies reserve direct mail advertising for prior customers. These companies build a list from the names and addresses of customers who have made purchases through other distribution channels. The response rate is significantly increased when advertising materials are directed at customers already familiar with your company and its goods and services.

[ ] This idea or its modification could work for my business.

#16 Direct Mail - Coupon Co-op Advertising

There are several companies listed in the Yellow Pages under "Advertising Direct Mail" that provide a co-op direct mail service especially effective for coupon advertising to consumers. These companies will design, typeset, print and mail your advertising piece or coupon along with several other non-competing coupon ads to residential homes in the areas of your choice. Each area usually covers approximately 10,000 homes and clients can have their advertising coupons sent to as many areas as desired. The advertising packs are generally put together and mailed six to eight times a year. The minimum order usually is one two-color coupon or advertising insert to 10,000 homes. The advantage of this approach is that the cost to mail your material is greatly reduced since it is combined with other advertiser's materials. If this advertising approach has promise for your company, have your coupon art work developed by a professional graphic designer, and ask for an allowance on the rate. Most co-op coupon distributors are simply salespersons. Even though they will claim to be able to design your piece, they have little knowledge or skill in creating effective coupon ads.

[ ] This idea or its modification could work for my business.

#17 Door Hangers

Announce a sale, special offering, grand opening or event with door hangers. Have your message printed on a heavy paper stock and die cut with a hole to slip on a door handle. Then, hire the local Boy Scout Troop, Little League team or Camp Fire group to distribute them door-to-door in the neighborhoods around your store, institution, office or territory. Be sure to print a credit line on the door hanger saying ....."This message delivered to you by the Boy Scout Troop #111." You'll get your message delivered with no effort and your donation to the organization for their delivery service will help with their fund raising efforts and establish some "good will" in the community you serve. If your company provides residential services such as carpet cleaning, roof repair, landscaping services or remodeling, have the service crew blanket the neighborhood with door hangers after each job. Since they are in the neighborhood anyway, they can easily do some door-to-door canvassing. Be sure to leave space on the hanger to write the address of the customer just served and suggest the neighbor ask them for a reference. This word-of-mouth advertising by satisfied cutomers, initiated by the door hanger, can produce lots of referrals.

[ ] This idea or its modification could work for my business.

#18 Fliers or Circulars

You can use fliers or circulars in hundreds of ways to promote your business. Put them in packages of customers, distribute in parking lots or door-to-door, put on bulletin boards, hand out at trade fairs and shows, mail alone or with other material, hand out on street corners and put in "Take One" racks. Circulars or fliers should tell the reader about special offers and stimulate interest in buying. Raise awareness, provide information and sell your goods and services with a simple flier. Make sure you list the benefits and features of the offer and give enough information about where to find it. Fliers also can be given to satisfied customers to pass on to their friends and family. Typeset or produce the flier art work on desk-top publishing and take it to a fast-print shop for production. Creating a half-page flier will allow you to print two on every sheet of paper and stretch your printing dollars without losing much impact.

[ ] This idea or its modification could work for my business.

#19 Letterhead

If you provide professional or business services, it is especially important for you to invest in good business stationery - letterhead, envelopes and business cards. Have a graphic designer develop a company logo and stationery design that is consistent with your company image. Many companies list their services on their letterhead to stimulate additional awareness and cross-selling opportunities. New consultants, usually middle managers or executives who've always had their expenses paid for by a corporation and are now on their own, are notorious for making a big mistake when they order their business stationery. To save money, they go to a fast-print shop and order the cheapest stuff available. They give little thought to the name of their business or its graphic image. Unfortunately, they use this cheap stationery to submit proposals seeking thousands of dollars in consulting fees. Then, they wonder why they don't get the work. Investing in good business stationery can be critical to the success of many service and professional companies. A company's business stationery usually leaves the recipient with its first and often lasting impression about the company.

[ ] This idea or its modification could work for my business.

#20 Postcards

Postcards are an easy and inexpensive way to announce an event, sale, or discount, or to serve as a coupon or reminder notice. Dentists and doctors have used them for years to remind patients about annual or semi-annual check-ups. Other service industries might do the same to encourage repeat business. Use postcards to thank customers for a referral or for their initial business. Postcards are easy to use and require less postage than a letter. They also can be sent first-class for less postage than bulk mail. Returned, first-class postcards can assist you in maintaining your mailing list and keeping it current. Print hundreds of postcards with your company logo, slogan or symbol on one side and leave the back side blank. Print at least enough to last a year. You can type or hand write messages as needed or take a quantity to a fast-print shop to print a special message or offer on the postcard. Some enterprising business owners print their newspaper or magazine ads on the back of their postcards and mail them to their customers. By so doing, they obtain double duty from their advertising art work.

[ ] This idea or its modification could work for my business.

#21 Statement Stuffers

If you regularly send statements to your customers, include a coupon, flier, ad re-print or announcement with the statement. Use statement stuffers to pitch new products and services, announce sales, provide discount coupons or announce sneak-preview sales for preferred customers. Never send a statement without an appeal to the customer to continue to buy. Occasionally a simple message included in the statement thanking the customer for his/her business also can go a long way toward increasing the loyalty of the customer. Some companies trade statement stuffers with non-competing businesses that have the same client base. With this approach, each company can benefit by reaching a wider audience with information about their goods and services at no extra distribution cost. Statement stuffers also can be used for direct marketing. By carefully designing the enclosure, the business owner can provide information about the product, make an offer to the customer and include an order form to make the sale. The order form can be returned with the customer's payment. What could be easier?

[ ] This idea or its modification could work for my business.

#22 Take One Racks

"Take One" racks are useful for distributing brochures and coupons. Put them in waiting rooms or on retail counters to stimulate interest or cross-sell other products and services. Exchange "Take-One" racks with companies offering compatible products or services to the same target market. Make sure you add a "Free" sign on the rack so people will be encouraged to pick up the literature. Add the words "Valuable Coupons" or "Special Offer" and you will sharply increase the distribution of the material in your "Take One" racks.

[ ] This idea or its modification could work for my business.

#23 Video Tapes

If your product or service can be demonstrated and explained better by using moving pictures, then you may wish to consider producing a short, 5-8 minute video tape as a sales tool. The video can be shipped to potential customers (using a deposit to ensure its return), used at trade fairs and shows, played at home demonstrations and showed at group presentations. The key to a great video tape is using it to walk the prospect through the sales process and to help him better understand how the product or service can meet his needs. A picture may be worth a thousand words, but a good video may be all you need to make the sale. Be sure you understand the customer's needs before you start production, and create a video that will stimulate demand and urgency to purchase. Contact local video production firms in your community for information on how to produce a video. New technology is making this method of advertising increasingly affordable.

[ ] This idea or its modification could work for my business.

REMINDER ADVERTISING

#24 Advertising Specialties

Items on which the name of the company and logo are imprinted and given to prospects or existing customers are called "advertising specialties" and are carried by companies listed in the Yellow Pages under that heading. Items include pens and pencils, key chains, paperweights, matches, ashtrays, coffee mugs, etc. Ad specialties are used to remind customers about your business, but are not much good if not carefully selected and used properly. They work best to increase the loyalty of valued customers or to keep your name in front of potential clients. In the case of existing customers or clients, the specialty should be of some significant value and should be given very discriminately. Small items like key chains and ballpoint pens can be successfully used as free gifts for grand openings, trade shows or other promotions. The elderly are especially attracted to these small, free items. A local bank in a prominent retirement community offered a free key chain with every deposit made on a certain day. Before the bank could open, customers were lined up around the block.

[ ] This idea or its modification could work for my business.

#25 Balloons

Use balloons to draw attention to your retail store or to add a festive touch to a special event. Have the company logo imprinted on the balloon and put clusters of helium filled balloons outside the store. Tie single balloons next to special sale items in the store to draw attention. Balloons also are very successful as give-aways at events that might attract parents and their children. Sales slogans also can be printed on the balloons. Use balloons for customer games and contests. For example, put vouchers good for prizes in selected, air-filled balloons attached to a board or wall and have customers break a balloon to see if they are a prize winner. Release helium-filled balloons with tags advertising your business. Include a balloon with a tag worth a valuable prize for the person finding the lucky balloon.

[ ] This idea or its modification could work for my business.

#26 Billboards

Billboards remind customers of your existence and usually must be accompanied with other forms of advertising to be effective. If you are running a month-long special sale and are using radio and print advertising to announce the event, billboards will work to remind people about the sale. Also, billboards can be effective if you can get the billboard closest to your establishment and put "next exit" or "right at the corner" on the sign. Use a maximum of six or less words and have the billboard designed to make a strong visual statement. One company successfully used a single billboard as the core of its image and positioning strategy. The billboard, located at a highly visible location, was rented by the same firm for years and always carried a dramatic photo of a lion accompanied by a clever slogan. The billboard was consistently a traffic stopper and worked well since the company's name is Lyon Realty. When the billboard was taken down to make way for a commercial development, the event was covered by every major newspaper and TV station in the community. The billboard had become a city landmark. In another case, a giant, round painting of a pizza was attached to a billboard advertising a local pizza chain. When youngsters stole it as a prank, the "case of the missing pizza" got front page coverage for 3 days. Sales at the pizza parlor soared. The youngsters were given free pizzas as a reward for returning the billboard section.

[ ] This idea or its modification could work for my business.

#27 Bumper Stickers

It is amazing that people will put bumper stickers on their cars to promote someone else's business. Bumper stickers seem to work especially well for radio stations and convenience stores. If you want to try bumper stickers to promote your business, tie your sticker promotion to a local sports team (you must get permission from the team first) and you are almost guaranteed a winner. You can use the bumper sticker to get foot traffic in the store by advertising a message such as "Pick up your Boston Celtics bumper sticker at your local ----- store and support the team" or "Get a free Blue Bombers bumper sticker with every purchase of -----." Be sure your company name or product logo is big enough to read from a car bumper. There are other tie-in possibilities for bumper stickers beyond sports, so use your imagination. Bumper stickers are useful for private schools, medical services and non-profit organizations, as well. Custom bumper stickers are available from advertising specialty companies and some local printers.

[ ] This idea or its modification could work for my business.

#28 Bus and Taxi Ads

Bus signs and taxi signs are best used in combination with other forms of advertising. They are used to remind customers and clients of your existence. They work best for companies located on a bus line or for special services that may appeal to bus riders. In some cases, bus and taxi signs can be used as a direct marketing method by including a tear-off coupon or response card to ad posters inside the vehicles. If your community has a trolley or special transportation vehicle for tourism, restaurants, hotels and fast food services located on the route might benefit from advertising on the vehicle.

[ ] This idea or its modification could work for my business.

#29 Bus Bench/Shelter Signs

This tool is best used with other advertising and serves to remind people of the existence of the business, product or event. Bus bench and bus shelter signs are most effective when placed as close as possible to the business. Because it is not a targeted advertising method, it best serves businesses that have a broad range of customers. Grocery stores, convenience stores, department stores or products like shampoo and toothpaste might consider bus bench signs. A restaurant on the same corner might use the bench sign as an additional invitation to "Step into Joe's Cafe for the Best Steak in Town," or "You've found Joe's Place, come on in."

[ ] This idea or its modification could work for my business.

#30 Buttons

Buttons are used most effectively with sales incentive programs for employees. Buttons can be given to employees that say things like, "Ask me about our special offer," or "Summer Sale July 4-9" or "Help me win a trip to Hawaii, I deserve it." These buttons can call additional attention to a special sales promotion and encourage the customer to open a conversation so the clerk or sales person can sell more goods or services. Buttons are a friendly ice breaker. You probably won't get your customers to wear your buttons, unless your company uses the buttons as part of a promotion with some charitable or civic event or issue. One store had good luck pinning on "I shopped 'til I dropped at (store's name) Spring Sale" buttons on every customer leaving the store. Since the store was located in a large shopping mall, the buttons stimulated additional traffic.

[ ] This idea or its modification could work for my business.

#31 Calendars

For years, calendars have been used successfully to keep the name of a business before customers the entire year. However, to work, an advertising calendar given by a business owner to a customer or prospect, must be worth keeping. Pocket and desk calendars, wall calendars and poster calendars all have been successful. You can get them from advertising specialty companies and office supply stores. Have your company name and logo imprinted on each calendar. Another option is to commission an original calendar or a series of calendars to be identified only with your business. This last option can be expensive and should be used only if the calendars will be one of the company's main forms of advertising. Do not give away cheap, ugly calendars! They will be tossed in the garbage as soon as they are received. Do it right, or save your money and don't do it at all.

[ ] This idea or its modification could work for my business.

#32 Decals

Decals fall in the same category as buttons, bumper stickers, symbols and outdoor advertising. They serve as a reminder to your customers or potential customers that you are still around and available to do business. The most effective use of decals is by MasterCard and Visa. The credit card companies supply the decals to be placed on the doors or windows of the merchants that use their credit card service. Colleges also have been successful in having students and alumni buy decals to place on their cars. If you supply a number of merchants with your products, you might want to consider developing a decal for them to use. For example, "Yummy Ice Cream Served Here," or "XYZ Insurance accepted here." In your other advertising, you can ask prospects to look for the decal in the window of participating merchants or service providers.

[ ] This idea or its modification could work for my business.

#33 Electronic Messages on Blimps and Planes

Some companies use blimps and airplanes to fly over large crowds gathered for outdoor evening events such as sporting events, concerts, night-time parades, etc. Advertising messages spelled out in electronic lights scroll across the bottom of the plane or the side of the blimp. This is not recommended for a business with a tight budget. However, this advertising vehicle works well when teamed with other forms of advertising and is best used by companies that already have a well established identity in the market. It can also work as teaser advertising. You can find these advertising services in the Yellow Pages.

[ ] This idea or its modification could work for my business.

#34 Exterior Building Signs

Customers will have difficulty locating a business if adequate signs are not used to identify the company. This is especially true for retail businesses. Not only is a good sign important in helping customers or clients find a business, it can serve as a powerful advertising tool to attract attention from passing motorists. While local building codes or sign ordinances may restrict the size and placement of the company sign, try to have the largest, most visible and highest quality sign you can afford placed in front of your business. Resist using hand-made signs or signs produced with stencils. Your business sign provides one of the first impressions your customer gets and sets the tone for your company's image. Light the sign and you will double its effectiveness. Even if your establishment is closed in the evening, a lighted sign can call attention to the business during night-time hours.

[ ] This idea or its modification could work for my business.

#35 Grocery Store Cart Signs

Many grocery store carts now carry frames to insert small advertising posters that will reach the shopper with a sales message while the shopper is pushing the cart around the store. If you have products sold in the store or are announcing a program, service or sale at a location near the store, consider this opportunity. Ask the store manager for information. The manager will be able to provide you with the information you need to explore this opportunity. If you decide this form of advertising is right for you, have your signs professionally printed or produced at a sign company. Keep them simple. The best placement is on the inside of the cart, so the sign and its message is in view every time the shopper places an item in the cart.

[ ] This idea or its modification could work for my business.

#36 Moving Billboards on Trucks

It is now possible to buy billboard space on large, semi-tractor trailer trucks that routinely cross the country. The advertiser pays for the space and the poster and the trucking firm guarantees to display the message for a certain period of time as the trucks travel along the highways and interstate routes. This method works well for goods and services with a national market. While it won't be responsible for immediate sales, this type of advertising can help increase public awareness about a company and/or its products. It should be used with other forms of advertising. If you have products used by truckers or the trucking industry, check this out.

[ ] This idea or its modification could work for my business.

#37 Place Mats

If you are located in a shopping center that has a popular restaurant, approach the owner and suggest that several of the businesses in the immediate area get together and purchase and print place mats for the restaurant free of charge. The restaraunt owner must be willing to let the place mats carry small ads about the participating businesses. One restaurant in a small town sells classified ad space on their place mats to local residents who want to buy, sell or trade personal items. Town folks come to the cafe regularly just to read and take home a place mat - after they have purchased a meal, of course. The owner prints new ones every two weeks, which helps to keep the customers coming back.

[ ] This idea or its modification could work for my business.

#38 Point-of-Purchase Signs

These are great for generating cross-selling opportunities or impulse buying. If point-of-purchase advertising signs are not available from the manufacturer or supplier of the products you are selling, make your own. Use a felt tip pen or stick-on letters to create signs that encourage customers to buy. For example, "Just $000," "This model features....," "Ask about our small business discount," "Free ... with purchase of ...," "On Sale Today," etc. These signs should be placed close to the merchandise they are referring to. Signs can help close the sale, since people are in the buying mood when they enter the store. Point-of-purchase signs also can be used in promoting personal services. Place them in the waiting rooms and seating areas to announce payment and credit policies, special promotions and other services you offer.

[ ] This idea or its modification could work for my business.

#39 Signs at Sporting Events

Sponsor a sign in the outfield of the Little League field or at other organized sporting events for youngsters or adults. This type of advertising vehicle also is available at professional or semi-professional sports arenas and stadiums, as well. The signs work especially well for goods or services a company wants associated with sports, health or fitness. The local business also will gain goodwill from the community for its participation in supporting the team. Ice cream and pizza parlors and children's clothing stores in the neighborhood of the Little League fields, have benefited from this form of advertising. A business owner can increase the effectiveness of the sign he sponsors by handing out samples, coupons or sales literature during the games.

[ ] This idea or its modification could work for my business.

#40 Telephone Hold Messages

If you frequently put customers or clients on hold when they telephone your business, you should consider adding a pre-recorded advertising message to your phone system. You can give information about your products and services, hours of operation or special company events. Customers can listen to a sales pitch while they wait for someone to answer the phone. Or, you can offer the listener useful information relative to your business or industry - information that will keep the caller from getting bored or angry while waiting. Some business owners use this method to tell the listener about their philosophy of doing business or their standards for customer service with a brief message. Production companies offer a service to professionally record your messages and install the system.

[ ] This idea or its modification could work for my business.

#41 Telephone Pole & Light Post Signs

If you have residential services to offer, like housecleaning, yard maintenance, plumbing, electrical repair, tree stump removal, piano lessons, window washing, tree trimming, tutoring, snow shoveling and pool cleaning, consider this method. Make some large, readable signs with the service you offer and a telephone number to call. Post the signs throughout your preferred service territory on light posts and telephone poles. The signs are especially effective if placed on posts located at the corner. That way, people coming from both directions can see them. This cheap and easy method has brought remarkable results for many small business owners. Do make sure that you are not contravening any laws first.

[ ] This idea or its modification could work for my business.

#42 T-Shirts

Imprinted T-shirts, like other ad specialties, serve to remind people of your existence. As often as T-shirts have been used as a business promotional method, they are still effective and everyone loves them. Use them as a special give-away or offer them free with the purchase of an item or service. They are especially effective if tied to a special promotional event or sponsorship. Also, T-shirts given to employees are great for morale. Some business owners use imprinted T-shirts as the company uniform. If you decide to use T-shirts as one of your marketing methods, be sure to get the best quality T-shirt you can afford and print the company's name and logo as large as possible, yet within good taste. The people who wear your T-shirts will become walking advertisements for your company.

[ ] This idea or its modification could work for my business.

#43 Vehicle Signs

Use your vehicle to promote your business. Large vehicles like trucks and vans should carry information about your goods and services, as well as the company name, logo and telephone number. Place your slogan on the side and back panels of the truck and paint your telephone number very large. The truck or van will act as a moving billboard. Magnetic signs promoting your business also can be purchased and placed on the doors of cars during business hours and removed when the car is in service for personal use. Vehicle signs are an inexpensive way to promote your business everytime you make a delivery or go on an appointment.

[ ] This idea or its modification could work for my business.

#44 Video Commercials at Checkout Counters

Check out counters at grocery stores will soon be carrying video tape playback machines that will run short commercials on the products and services available in the store and in the neighborhood. This would be a good vehicle to consider if you are selling to a mass market or if your offering is best explained through demonstration. You may wish to produce a short video for use at your store counter, office waiting area or shop office. The video tapes can be used to demonstrate, educate, explain, inform and sell. They are especially efffective if customers must wait for service. While they wait, they can learn about your goods and services. A good video tape is like a magnet; it captures the viewer's full attention.

[ ] This idea or its modification could work for my business.

ATTENTIONGETTERS

#45 Loudspeaker Announcements

Consider using a loudspeaker system in your retail store to announce special offerings and encourage sales. K-Mart's "blue light special" is a good example of how to generate excitement and urgency with a loudspeaker and get people to buy items they may not have had in mind when they entered the store. First, identify a number of items you wish to move and be willing to seriously discount the price. You might offer two items for the price of one or provide some other sales incentive or price slashing discount to create urgency. On your peak traffic days, periodically announce the items and then give a time limit for customers to take advantage of the offer. Identify the location of the items with a helium balloon, flag, large sign or flashing light.

[ ] This idea or its modification could work for my business.

#46 Picket Your Establishment

Pay individuals to picket your establishment with signs that draw attention to your products, services and special prices. Use your children and their friends, if necessary. Make sure the signs are large. Use big, dark letters on the signs so passengers in passing cars can read them. This activity can call attention to a sale or new product, especially if the signs are particularly clever. If you call the photo desk of the newspaper in advance of the event, you might land a photo in a local newspaper, as well.

[ ] This idea or its modification could work for my business.

#47 Search Lights

Search lights can be rented to attract attention to a special sale, grand opening or special event. Search lights are an attention-getting ploy to obtain greater awareness about the location of your store, office complex, factory or warehouse. If you think you might like to try a search light, you can maximize the effectiveness by shining it on something unusual, such as a large inflatable King Kong on the roof, a helium balloon in an unusual shape, or a sign with a clever saying. If you do any of these things, be sure to alert the news media and attempt to get publicity coverage of the event. Search lights are great for calling attention to a late-night sale or after-hours factory tour. Sales such as a "midnight madness sale" can draw unusually large crowds for the right kind of merchandise. Water bed retailers and record/tape stores have done well with this late-hour promotion, helped by the search light. Be sure to mention in other advertising that customers should follow the search light to the store for the special offering, grand opening, anniversary event or factory tour.

[ ] This idea or a modification could work for my business.

#48 Sidewalk Signs

Place "A" frame signs on the sidewalk in front of the store to tell people you are "OPEN" or to announce a "SALE" or special event. Be sure you do not place the signs directly in the way of pedestrians. Chalkboard "A" frame signs are effective for businesses that wish to publicize daily specials. They have worked well for restaurants, bookstores and liquor shops. The purpose of the sidewalk sign is to get the attention of people passing by. Obviously, they work only if the store has a reasonable amount of sidewalk foot traffic.

[ ] This idea or its modification could work for my business.

#49 Signs Draped on the Building

Large signs or banners can be draped temporarily on a building to announce a "Grand Opening," "Summer Sale," "Now Leasing" or new product line..."Xxx Is Here." Hang the fabric signs as close to the top of the building as possible. The higher the sign, the more visible it will be. A sign on a twelve-story building will naturally attract more attention than a sign on a one-story building. Make sure the lettering is large enough to be easily read from a distance. You also can consider hanging banners out the windows or draping a large American flag on the side of a building to get attention.

[ ] This idea or its modification could work for my business.

#50 Signs & Banners Towed by Airplanes

A large sign or banner carrying your message can be towed behind an airplane to places where crowds gather. You see this often at the beach. One beer manufacturing company towed a large, cloth replica of a beer can behind a plane along a California beach on a holiday weekend. It received the full attention of every thirsty beach goer for miles along the shore. Another time, a helicopter towed a sports car followed by an airplane towing a sign saying "Win this car, listen to XXXX radio." It also got attention. In yet another example, a candidate for public office hired a plane to buzz over an open stadium during an NFL football game. The plane towed a sign urging people to elect the candidate. Again, this form of advertising is like billboards and search lights; it is great as a reminder or attention-getter, but should not be used alone. If you are thinking about using such approaches, be sure to run print ads in the local paper the same day or have someone hand out coupons, fliers or samples to the crowd. Generally speaking, large companies can employ these kind of activities because they have big budgets and can support a variety of advertising and promotional vehicles, including these outrageous gimmicks. However, don't rule out such a method if you have a product or service that might lend itself to this kind of promotion. You also may be able to generate lots of free publicity, if your approach is original. Be sure to notify the news media of your activity in advance. You will have to carefully plan this promotion and work very hard to make this activity pay off. Nevertheless, the attention you could receive may very well be all it takes to launch your business. You can locate these advertising services in the Yellow Pages.

[ ] This idea or its modification could work for my business.

#51 Skywriters

If you live in a climate where skywriting will work and if you are having an annual event or launching a new product that you are advertising in a variety of ways, consider hiring a skywriter. Skywriting can work to draw additional attention to the event or product. It is another reminder that you are having your annual anniversary sale, grand opening of a new store, or introduction of a new product. Alone, skywriting like other attention-getters is not effective and should not be considered. But once in a while, for a special promotional event and in combination with several other advertising methods, it can help support a sales campaign and get the public talking about your business. Skywriters can be found in the Yellow Pages.

[ ] This idea or its modification could work for my business.

#52 Symbols

You can draw attention to your company by creating and using a symbol. A western wear store has a life-size horse hitched to a post in front of the store. An autobody repair shop has a beat-up car on the roof of its shop. A liquor company has a two-story inflatable replica of one of the products it offers and uses it at a variety of places. A pest control company has a large black spider riding on top of all the company vehicles. Ronald McDonald represents the McDonald's Restaurant chain. Remember Jack-in-the-Box and the Planter's Peanut man? These symbols help identify a company, distinguish it from its competitors and remind people the business is still around. If you are considering a symbol for your company, pick one that makes sense and that has a timeless quality to it. Then, use it with all your advertising and promotional activites.

[ ] This idea or its modification could work for my business.

#53 Walking Signs

Hire a student or model to walk down a crowded beach or on a busy street with a sandwich board sign, advertising your company or its products or services. This technique will be even more effective if the person in the sandwich board hands out fliers, brochures, samples or coupons. The person must be friendly and able to provide information about where to obtain your goods or services. The sign should be easy to read from a distance. Be sure to make the wording on the sign as clever as possible. To gain additional attention, consider putting the individual in an appropriate costume. If you can't afford to hire a model or student, get your family members involved.

[ ] This idea or its modification could work for my business.

#54 Window Signs

Put large, simple signs in your window to announce a sale, special offering or special event. This works best when combined with other advertising and promotional activities. However, it is a big mistake to have a permanent "sale" sign in the store window. After a month or two, customers and those passing by will not believe the message and the store will lose credibility. One of the most effective users of simple, paper window signs have been grocery stores. For years, they've put signs advertising their weekly specials in the store windows. The signs work to bring in customers and move merchandise. Service businesses can consider this approach, as well. One savings and loan association hires a local artist to paint holiday designs and greetings on the lobby windows, along with current rates for deposits. Many dry cleaners and beauty salons also have used window signs effectively to promote their services. If store window signs are a possibility for you, remember to make them easy to read from a distance and to change them frequently.

[ ] This idea or its modification could work for my business.

CHAPTER TWO

PACKAGING

Beauty may be only skin deep, but there is nothing more attractive than a beautiful woman or a handsome man. These individuals usually get our initial attention and only afterward do we discover if there is any substance behind the "pretty face."

The same principle holds true in marketing. The packaging of a product can be critical to its success. A product may never see the light of day if the packaging doesn't motivate the consumer to buy it, take it home, open the package and use it.

Put very simply, packaging is the wrapping, box, bag or container that surrounds the product. It serves two purposes - to protect the product and to convey an image. The packaging of a product can be the critical difference between whether someone selects your product or your competitor's product, especially if you must fight for shelf space and attention.

In the case of a service, packaging can be considered the context in which the service is delivered. For example, a bank's environment, including office design and decoration, serves as the "package" for its financial services. Service companies also should try to make their service tangible to the customer in some way. For instance, an insurance company may wish to "package" its insurance documents in a nice folder for the customer's safekeeping.

Depending on the target market, the type of packaging will have varying degrees of importance. Generally speaking, the more up-scale the product, the more attention you should pay to the package.

Unfortunately, many small companies try to contain costs by cutting corners on the packaging. That may be a terrible mistake, because the decision to buy or not to buy a product is often based on the appeal of the package that contains it. That's why some companies spend more money on the package than on the product itself.

When making packaging decisions, small or emerging companies with limited resources may have to start with stock packaging or spartan environments rather than custom packaging and lavish surroundings. Even so, the variety and quality of stock packaging has improved over the years and a semi-custom look can be achieved with a little imagination. Office environments can have a clean and efficient look no matter how modest. Once your product shows evidence that it will be successful, you can consider investing in custom packaging or professional interior office design to enhance the appeal of your goods or services. Be sure to employ a professional package designer to help you.

One good approach is to consider the package design at the same time the product is being developed. Packaging should not be an afterthought or a last-minute decision. Think about your product and try to cover all the details that can be involved in the packaging before you start designing the wrapper or container. For example, will your packaging require tamper-proof devices, bar codes, or product liability information? Have you also considered the shipping requirements, ease of opening, display requirements and shop worn prevention aspects of the packaging?

Whenever possible, let your packaging promote your business. Use the packaging to carry information about other products and services you offer and sales messages. Your packaging should not only convey an image, it should help sell the product. The packaging can announce discounts or special offers, give information about the benefits and features of the product, give the location of your business, provide a telephone number for additional orders and carry your company logo.

Careful attention must be paid to packaging because many customers will buy on impulse when they are attracted to the package.

Finally, if your product is not successful in one package, try it in another before you abandon it completely.

#55 Envelopes

Print sales messages on your envelopes. Announce special promotions and offers that are detailed on the inside by printing teaser messages on the outside of the envelope. Always print your logo and company name on the outside, as well. If you cannot afford to print custom envelopes, purchase a rubber stamp with your logo and return address. Then, stamp all your plain envelopes. In addition, rubber stamps with messages like "Special Offer Inside," and "Open Immediately," can be purchased and used to draw attention to your mail.

[ ] This idea or its modification could work for my business.

#56 Folders and Binders

If you are in a service industry and provide documents to your customers, you can make the service more tangible by placing the documents in a quality folder or binder with your company's name and logo printed, embossed or foil stamped on the cover. If you are charging several hundred to several thousand dollars for consulting services, clients will feel better about the cost and the service if they receive a quality folder or binder in which to keep the documents. Don't skimp on the folders or binders, because doing so will reflect a negative image. On the inside cover of the folder or binder, print a brief statement about your company and its philosophy of service. Then, list all the services you offer. This will increase the potential for future business and cross-selling of other services. Don't assume that if the customer buys one service from you that he/she is aware of all your other services. Use your packaging to promote your business and enhance its image. This is especially easy to do with folders and binders.

[ ] This idea or its modification could work for my business.

#57 Mailing Labels

If you do a lot of mailing, make sure your logo and address are printed on all your mailing labels. Better yet, enlarge the labels and make room for your best advertising slogan, as well. This is an easy and effective way to reinforce your marketing messages. Some business owners who do a high volume of mail order business change the advertising message on their labels every month.

[ ] This idea or its modification could work for my business.

#58 Package Inserts

Advertise your other products or services by including your brochures, fliers, coupons, ad reprints, mail order catalogs and other sales materials in your packages. This works for both retail and mail order companies. It also works for service companies who give out sales materials at the time the service is rendered. Package inserts are great for announcing an upcoming sale, a special promotion or a public relations event. They also can be used to alert customers to a line of products or services they may not know your company provides. Also, consider exchanging package inserts with a non-competing company that has the same target market. By doing so you can extend your advertising reach with little extra cost or effort. Both companies can benefit from this kind of promotional arrangement and both companies can save on their advertising costs. Package inserts make good sense. Since you have already sold something to the customer, it is very likely he/she will purchase from you again. Package inserts also are an easy way to encourage repeat sales. The main point to remember is to never let a package leave the business without including an advertising insert that encourages the customer to buy from you again.

[ ] This idea or its modification could work for my business.

#59 Print on the Box/Container

Print key sales messages on the box or container of your product. Use words like, "guaranteed," "easy to use," "new," "revolutionary," "saves you money," etc. to attract attention to the product. This is especially important if the product must compete for attention with lots of other products on the shelf. Let the package help sell the merchandise in it. In addition, print messages on bags and wrappers. Again, don't settle for a plain, brown paper bag. Print your name and logo on the package and include messages that will encourage repeat business.

[ ] This idea or its modification could work for my business.

#60 Stickers

Print stickers with your company logo or name and your telephone number on them. Attach your stickers to products leaving the store. For example, a retail computer store owner attaches his sticker on every computer or printer that leaves the business. He tells customers to call if they have any questions and to use the sticker as a handy reference. The customer always has a visible reminder of the store where the purchase was made and can easily refer another potential customer. Don't skimp on the stickers. Make sure the sticker is attractive. If they look tacky, the customer will simply remove them. Also, place "On Sale" or "20% OFF" stickers on products you have marked down. You also can use stickers to add new sales messages to your promotional materials. For example, if you discover another use for your product, announce it with a sticker - "Can be used as..." Finally, colorful stickers make great give away items for businesses that sell children's products or services.

[ ] This idea or its modification could work for my business.

#61 Tape or Ribbon

Some clever entrepreneurs have symbols, logos, and sales messages printed on packaging tape or ribbon to remind the customer about where he/she bought the product. This technique is especially useful for businesses that ship products to customers who stock the items over a period of time. If the purchasing agent should leave the business, no one will have to guess about who supplied the products - it's on the packaging tape. It's a good idea to print your mailing address and telephone number on the tape, as well.

[ ] This idea or its modification could work for my business.

CHAPTER THREE

PERSONAL SALES

Personal sales methods take place when the business owner or the company's sales force make direct, eyeball-to-eyeball appeals to potential customers or to referral sources in an effort to drum up business and create selling opportunities.

Personal sales methods are by far the most effective promotional techniques, simply because they are so personal. They create an opportunity for the buyer and seller to come in direct contact and to establish a relationship. These methods are especially important in the service industry, where trust and confidence in the provider is required to close the sale.

Nevertheless, personal sales methods are the most costly in time spent per customer. Therefore, business owners should use personal sales techniques for potential customers on their most preferred prospect list and avoid using these approaches on lower priority customers or prospects.

Love may make the world go 'round, but sales will make the business survive. Whether you are responsible for doing your own selling or have an organized sales force, attention to the sales process is critical to business success.

To help you do a better job managing your sales effort, some direction, management and control must be used to make sure the money and time allocated to personal selling is wisely spent.

Set Objectives

Set some objectives for the sales effort. Besides selling, the effort also should include prospecting for new clients or customers, communicating useful information about your business to the customer, following up with customer service and gathering information for use in product and management decision-making.

Develop a Prospect List

Prospecting is used to identify potential buyers, as well as discover their needs, wants, likes and dislikes. Here the quality of the prospect list is more important than its length. Building the prospect list is one of the most valuable activities of the sales process. Everyone associated with the business should be prospecting for new customers. A good prospect is one that needs and wants what the company offers and also is able to buy. Qualify prospects as much as possible to avoid wasting time and money on those that will never be in a position to buy your goods and services.

Stress the Benefits

One very big mistake many small business owners make is being too close to their packaged goods or services. The owner always can explain every feature and detail about how the item or service works, what sizes and colors it comes in, and how the item is produced or the service is delivered. The business owner often has the same proud enthusiasm as a new parent.

Unfortunately, the customer rarely cares, unless any or all of those features can be translated into direct benefits the consumer will receive when making the purchase.

People buy benefits and solutions to problems, not goods and services. For example, people do not buy statistical reports, they buy applications of data. They don't buy life insurance, they buy security and peace of mind. Put yet another way, they don't buy toasters, they buy an easy way to make toast.

Successful small business owners usually have what is called "customer-centered marketing." They have developed a rapport between the company and the customer. They completely understand the needs and concerns of the customer. They know what bothers the prospect, what problems need solving and what goals the prospect hopes to achieve when making the purchasing decision.

The business owner who really understands his/her customers will develop goods and services to meet their needs and solve their problems and use personal selling techniques to make the sale.

When you are developing or assessing your products, list the features and then determine how your customer benefits directly from each feature. Features include such things as size, style, brand name, quality, packaging, after-sale service, delivery, warranty, credit, installation and alteration. Check your product to see if it has the features that will give the customer the benefits he/she is looking for. If not, add the features that will make your product or service irresistible to the prospect.

Then, promote the benefits and not the features. In other words, let the prospect know exactly what's in it for him to buy from you and not your competitor. For example:

"You'll have nothing to lose with our unconditional guarantee."

"You'll find the exact color to enhance your image from our wide selection of colored shirts."

"You'll save money, because our top quality products are made to last."

The essence of successful marketing is understanding your customer's needs, providing goods and services that satisfy those needs and explaining to the prospect the benefits derived from purchasing your offering. Personal sales methods provide the most powerful way to do that.

#62 Business Networking

Join leads clubs, business networking groups, and trade associations to develop business leads and opportunities. You will need to be selective and determine which groups merit your time. Look for organizations with members serving the same target markets as your business and give each organization a six- to twelve-month trial period. These organizations can provide opportunities to do personal selling, expand your referral base and generate solid business leads. It is a good idea to prepare a brief "30-second commercial" and a 10-minute presentation about your company. If necessary, write your "commercial" on a 3" x 5" inch card and carry it with you. Always be prepared to give your "standard pitch."

[ ] This idea or its modification could work for my business.

#63 Business Lunches

There is no such thing as a free lunch and that is why business lunches work so well. Business lunches make great vehicles for personal selling. To successfully use the business lunch, plan ahead and determine what you want to accomplish. Do you want to make a sale, have a door opened or establish a referral source. Be clear about what you want and start the subject immediately after placing the lunch orders. Even if the lunch is "unsuccessful" the guest "owes you one" and may be helpful in the future. However, the guest cannot be helpful to your business if you have not clearly communicated what you need from him now, or in the future. If you know a client, business associate or key prospect is the type of personality who responds favorably to a free lunch, make a habit of taking that person to lunch from time to time, just to ask for feedback and to cement the relationship.

[ ] This idea or its modification could work for my business.

#64 Demonstrations

If a picture is worth a 1,000 words then a demonstration is worth more than a 100 pictures. If you can show your prospects how your product works and how it does exactly what you say it will do, you are more likely to sell it. Because seeing is believing, demonstrations can be your most effective sales presentation. A demonstration allows the viewer to witness the product in action. Prospects see for themselves just how they, too, can achieve the same results from the product. Through a demonstration, the product sells itself. People will gather around someone who is showing how to use the latest vegetable slicer or exercise equipment, because people just love to see how things work. If your product lends itself to show and tell, find places where potential customers gather and put on a demonstration. Shopping malls, retail stores, swap meets, trade shows, fairs, the beach and sports events are all possible locations. Always bring along sales material and products to sell, as well as an assistant to handout material, gather leads or take orders. If you are selling your product wholesale to retailers, arrange to have a demonstration at your manufacturing plant or show room.

[ ] This idea or its modification could work for my business.

#65 Home Parties

A number of products and services have been successfully sold and distributed through home demonstration parties. A hostess with an incentive to "earn merchandise" invites friends and acquaintances to the home for a "free demonstration" of products, which can be ordered on the spot. This approach has worked for household items, cosmetics, crystal, art work, jewelry and lingerie. If you have a product or service that is attractive to women, consider this approach.

[ ] This idea or its modification could work for my business.

#66 Door-to-Door Canvassing

Canvassing is the process of seeking out prospective customers and asking for their business. These cold calls are difficult because you only have a few seconds to establish a positive relationship. Try to find something in common with the prospect by talking about something other than the business. Then, give your pitch and ask for the business, or leave the door open for follow-up. By writing or calling prospects first and carefully targeting them, you can improve your chances for success with this method. Always leave a business card. Giving free demonstrations or samples when canvassing can help too. If you have a new office or store in a neighborhood and provide general consumer products or services, canvass the neighborhood, introduce yourself and invite your new neighbors to the grand opening. Leave fliers or announcements at each stop.

[ ] This idea or its modification could work for my business.

#67 Personal Letters

Personal letters work best for highly targeted markets. Short, clear personal letters are an inexpensive and effective marketing tool. First, learn about your prospective customers so you can personalize the letter and proposal as much as possible. Then, be sure to follow-up. Write another letter in a few weeks or follow with a phone call. The follow-up activity clearly demonstrates that the first letter was not a mass mail effort and that you are specifically interested in soliciting the prospect's business. Perhaps you may need to employ a two, three or four letter campaign. You should write the entire series of letters at one time to ensure continuity. Multiple mailings build customer confidence and familiarity.

[ ] This idea or its modification could work for my business.

#68 Proposals

Consultants often use proposals to sell a client on their service. The key to a successful proposal is first to understand the needs and wants of the client. This can be done by interviewing the prospect to determine the goals and objectives of the organization and their immediate needs and concerns. Then, demonstrate how the service you provide will meet those needs and wants in a carefully crafted proposal. Finally, be sure to package the proposal so that it projects confidence and credibility. One of the biggest mistakes new consultants make is using cheap materials and a sloppy format for their proposals. Invest in the "packaging" of the proposal, so that it has impact. Present the proposal at a business lunch or another occasion where the prospect can get to know you and develop confidence and trust in your ability to deliver the service you have outlined in your proposal.

[ ] This idea or its modification could work for my business.

#69 Sales Calls

Personal sales calls to highly profitable prospects can be very effective. Advanced preparation with scheduled appointments, sales materials and a motivating sales pitch are essential for success. Because personal sales calls take lots of time, they should only be used with selected, potentially high-profit customers. Sometimes it takes several calls to get the sale. Persistence pays. Often the business owner gives up just when they are finally close to landing a sale. If you have a few prospects you really want on your client list, staying in frequent touch is a clear way to let the prospect know you really want the business.

[ ] This idea or its modification could work for my business.

#70 Talks & Presentations

Short talks and presentations before business and client groups can be an easy way to sell yourself and your products or services. These mini-performances give the audience a chance to sample your ability. They position the speaker as an authority in the field and provide an opportunity to establish credibility and trust. Always give 10-15 minutes of useful information followed by a short question-and-answer period. Just before you conclude, give a "commercial" about your business and ask for business cards from those who might be interested in receiving more information from your company in the future. Put the leads from the business cards on your prospect list and follow up with other promotional methods.

[ ] This idea or its modification could work for my business.

#71 Telemarketing

For the small business owner, telemarketing usually means sales calls made by the owner or a staff member of the business to the prospect. Less expensive than an in-person sales call or a letter, telemarketing can be useful as part of an overall sales campaign. To be effective, however, the business owner should target prospects carefully and use telemarketing with other forms of promotion such as personal letters, direct mail, and print advertising. In addition, the caller must be prepared for a large number of rejections. Boiler room telemarketing operations are available through firms specializing in telephone sales. If you are considering this route, set up a small in-house telemarketing effort first to test the results before a firm is hired or an in-house boiler room is established. If the results of the test are poor, the cost of telemarketing may not warrant the effort and expense.

[ ] This idea or its modification could work for my business.

#72 Trade Fairs/ Product Exhibitions

Display, demonstrate and sell products and services at trade shows, fairs and exhibits. This approach requires a good display, excellent sales techniques and lots of enthusiasm. Review the publication, *Trade Show/Convention Guide*, available in your local library, to learn which shows might be the best place to display your products. If the cost of the booth rental is too high, find a business owner with a compatible product or service and share one booth. Be prepared to sell your product at the booth, not just display it. Remember, you are at the fair or trade show to make sales. Bring your order forms and credit card imprinter. Have a "free drawing" to obtain business cards to use as leads for future contacts and position someone at the entrance to hand out fliers to get foot traffic to your booth. Also, trade shows and fairs are wonderful places to pick up sales representatives for your products.

[ ] This idea or its modification could work for my business.

#73 Free Seminars

If you are in the service business, seminars can be especially effective in identifying interested customers and giving them a sales pitch. The program should last only an hour and be scheduled at a time most convenient to potential customers. Spend 40 minutes giving useful information on the subject. This will establish the credibility and authority of the speaker. Then spend 5 minutes on the sales pitch and leave the remaining time for questions and answers. End the session and be sure to have sales people ready to immediately close sales or make appointments with interested people.

[ ] This idea or its modification could work for my business.

CHAPTER FOUR

PUBLIC RELATIONS & PUBLICITY

Public relations activities attempt to raise public awareness and gain acceptance and support for a company and its goods and services through means other than paid advertising. Public relations methods include news releases and media relations, sponsorship of special events, charitable benefits, newsletters, thank-you letters, greeting cards and other activities.

Publicity is a public relations function that attempts to raise public awareness through articles and stories in the news media. Though it is difficult to control how the message is conveyed or the vehicle by which it is transmitted, carefully executed publicity programs can be very effective and results often can be achieved at a much lower cost than paid advertising. Today, it is even possible to target the message to potential customers by carefully selecting the media outlets.

Publicity can increase general awareness and help sales, especially in the case of new product launches. Other publicity and public relations activities are aimed at enhancing image and creating awareness and goodwill in a company's community and among a company's potential customers, employees, vendors, regulators and neighbors. Public relations activities generally should be undertaken as part of a company's long-range positioning strategy.

Public relations activities can never be used successfully to cover up bad policy or unethical business practices. Good public relations must start with the business owner's philosophy of doing business. That philosophy flows through the company's policies, procedures and practices. A company's day-to-day business operations often speak clearly for themselves. Public relations deals with reality, not smoke and mirrors.

With that in mind, public relations activities can be used to understand and influence the opinions of groups of people the company depends upon for success. Through these activities, a company can gain support for its position and be seen as a necessary and welcomed part of the community it serves.

For example, some small companies with strong, loyal followings have successfully battled government regulators or local agencies whose decisions might have put them out of business. They took their cases to the court of public opinion through the news media, letter writing campaigns and demonstrations and won reversals of bad decisions. These actions would never have happened if the companies had not cultivated their support groups with good public relations well in advance. Because they were viewed as an asset to the community, others were willing to stand up for them.

For your long-term success, be sure to include some public relations activities in your overall promotion plan.

#74 Charitable Events

Charitable giving is as much a part of America as is the free enterprise system. So, participating in the right charitable events can prove to be a "win-win" situation for many businesses and charities. For example, a fashionable, up-scale men's clothing store sponsored a cocktail hour and informal fashion show one Friday evening in the Fall. The event was called a "Friday Fall Fashion Fling." Tickets were ten dollars and all proceeds went to a home for runaway youth, of which the store owner was a volunteer member of the governing board. Refreshments were donated and T-shirts commemorating the event were sold. Members of the governing board of the home were all "yuppies" and of course, they were responsible for selling tickets to the event. They invited all their yuppie friends who packed the store. All those in attendance had a good time and got more than their money's worth of happy-hour food and drink. The store owner donated a sport coat for a prize drawing. The charity profited and so did the store owner when many in the crowd returned to buy thousands of dollars of clothing. The key to success with these kinds of promotional events is to make sure the event, sponsored by the business, will attract potential customers or clients, as well as support a worthwhile charity. With careful planning, everyone comes out a winner. As another example, a chain of weight control centers donated a penny to a local children's hospital for every pound their clients lost during a 6-month campaign. A picture of huge glass containers filled with pennies being presented to the hospital was printed in the local papers and was a visual testament to the success of the weight control program. The weight control centers signed up many new customers following the publicity they received for their charitable donation. Of course, business owners should believe in the charities they are supporting, or customers and friends will soon discover their motives are less than charitable.

[ ] This idea or its modification could work for my business.

#75 Charitable Giving

Direct giving to charitable organizations also can be a powerful tool to create goodwill and acceptance in the community. Charitable giving should be a part of every business budget, even if the budget is modest. Select charities that are personally important to the donor or the employees of a company. If the gift is substantial or significant to the charity, try to acquire some publicity or recognition for the gift, so that others will learn of your company's contribution to the community. Small businesses can be very creative in their giving. For example, the employees of one small business adopted a less fortunate family during the holiday season and provided them with food, clothing, gifts and housewares. Their efforts made a nice feature article in the local newspaper and their act of charity brought the employee team closer together. Other companies have donated their products or services to non-profit, social service agencies. One manufacturer of children's backyard playground equipment donates a complete set to one local children's program every year. The gift is welcomed and the company is viewed as a generous, civic-minded organization.

[ ] This idea or its modification could work for my business.

#76 Community Involvement

Another way to make your company visible and develop valuable contacts is to get involved in community development. Joining service organizations, serving on boards of directors for non-profit institutions and encouraging your employees to be active in community activities can help promote your business. In addition, service in these organizations can develop the leadership and organizational skills of your employees - skills that can prove to be useful in the management of the company.

[ ] This idea or its modification could work for my business.

#77 Employee Events

Company picnics, Christmas parties, employee bowling leagues and recreational opportunities can help instill loyalty and pride among employees of a company. When possible and appropriate, it is very helpful to invite the entire employee's family to these events so spouses and children can be better informed about the business. Family members who have enjoyed themselves at the expense of the company, often become the company's best promoters.

[ ] This idea or its modification could work for my business.

#78 Free Information

Develop an information piece and offer it free. The pamphlet or brochure should identify problems or concerns common among your customers and provide useful, "no-strings-attached" information to help solve the problems. The approach can be used by almost every business concern. A roofing inspector offers a brochure called "21 Ways to Avoid a Roofing Rip-Off." An office supply store offers a simple booklet called "10 Office Management Techniques for Top-notch Performance." A travel agent offers "Tips from the Experts for Travelling in Europe." People who request the brochure are always grateful for the free information. It also establishes the business as an authority in the field - a generous authority willing to share knowledge. In addition, when you offer a free brochure as a public service, you usually can get the news media to help you publicize your offer. The business owner can put the names and addresses of prospects who've requested the information on a mailing list for later follow-up.

[ ] This idea or its modification could work for my business.

#79 Grand Openings/ Anniversary Celebrations

Plan a grand opening celebration to announce a new business, a new location, or an expansion of existing business. The purpose is to call attention to the business, identify the location and create interest in what the company sells. Grand openings can be simple or elaborate affairs. You may need to support the grand opening with media advertising, a sign on the store, search lights and other activities. A physician, attorney, accountant or other professional service provider may find a direct mail announcement and an announcement in the newspaper to be sufficient. Remember, a grand opening event is to attract customers, not entertain family and friends. This is a good time to offer free food and small gifts imprinted with the company logo and location. Promote special merchandise, offer discounts, provide samples, conduct tours and give demonstrations, if appropriate, at the grand opening. The event can be duplicated for significant anniversaries. Such events must be supported by other advertising methods to let people know about the event and to entice them to come.

[ ] This idea or its modification could work for my business.

#80 Greeting Cards

Greeting cards can be an excellent public relations tool. Christmas cards, however, sometimes get lost with all the hoopla of the season and the enormous number of cards that pour in from other business owners. So, you might consider choosing another holiday, perhaps Thanksgiving or the first day of Spring to send a greeting card to your best customers thanking them for their business and continued support. Birthday or anniversary cards to individual customers are effective for companies providing personal and special services such as hairdressers, florists, jewelers, etc. A jeweler might record the wedding date of all couples buying engagement or wedding rings, being careful to record the new, permanent address of the couple. Then, about three weeks before the first anniversary, the jeweler could send an anniversary card. Of course, it will serve as a reminder to get a gift. Dentists and physicians have sent their patients birthday cards and other business owners have found this to be effective, as well. The purpose of the cards is to encourage customer loyalty and additional sales. They also serve to remind customers that you are thinking of them on their special day.

[ ] This idea or its modification could work for my business.

#81 Memberships in Organizations

Join the Chamber of Commerce and other business organizations that could be helpful in facilitating your business growth. These organizations are structured to help each business owner or representative make contacts to promote their business. Of course, these organizations are only as good as their leadership and if after a year or so they are not bringing results, you may wish to drop out. Nevertheless, you must be an active member to benefit from any group. Don't simply pay your dues, hang your plaque on the wall and expect things to happen. To gain from membership, a business owner must take time to get involved with activities that will provide opportunities for networking and business relationships to naturally develop. Membership in business organizations is especially useful for the business that depends on referrals. The contacts made through these organizations can be vital if a business owner ever needs to rally support for a cause from other business associates.

[ ] This idea or its modification could work for my business.

#82 News Releases

Send a brief, one-page, double-spaced information sheet to the news media to announce new products, a new location, business milestones or appointments of new key personnel. Also use news releases to attempt to get general publicity about your company. Try to seize every opportunity to keep your name in front of the public through the news media. The news media, especially your local newspapers and magazines, can help create familiarity and credibility for your business. Also appear on radio and TV talk shows if appropriate, and give useful information to the consumer. Working with the media can enhance the credibility of business owners and help establish them as the local experts in their fields. A news release is the best method to approach the media with newsworthy information, but don't rule out a quick telephone call to a reporter or the news desk with an item that might get their attention.

[ ] This idea or its modification could work for my business.

#83 Newsletters

Newsletters are effective for service professionals like attorneys, health care providers, accountants and financial consultants. Newsletters can keep you in touch with your customers and give your business instant credibility. You can sell services through your newsletter in a professional and dignified manner. Newsletters also are good for developing new customers or clients by mailing them to selected prospects. Mailed on a regular basis, they can be very effective in generating new business. Newsletters, however, can be time consuming and costly to design, write, print and mail. In addition, you must make a commitment to publishing a newsletter at least quarterly and for a year or two before you can honestly measure the results. Some companies produce generic newsletters for professional services that can be personalized with a local firm's name and address. These are available at much less cost, but are not specific to the firm and its services. Other companies offer semi-custom newsletters that provide space for a business owner to insert specific information about his/her business. The most effective newsletters are ones that are specific to the business - newsletters in which the owner controls all the information in the publication. The whole idea of a newsletter is to pass along useful, important information to your customers and prospects, establish yourself as an authority and build trust and confidence. After a few editions of your newsletter, a recipient begins to recognize it immediately and often looks forward to getting it. When prospects need what you offer, they will think of you first.

[ ] This idea or its modification could work for my business.

#84 Personalities

Sometimes associating your product or service with a personality or celebrity can increase sales. Because most small business owners can not afford a nationally known figure to represent them, they may find suitable personalities in the community. A radio announcer, college coach, TV weatherman, local athlete, politician, or a beauty queen may be just what your business could use to gain attention. The personality can endorse your products in your advertising. You can pay them to appear at a special event, such as a grand opening, major sale, charity event, etc. When you make it possible for people to meet a celebrity in person, they often respond by becoming loyal customers. If you decide to use a personality at an event, remember the purpose is to increase foot traffic and sales, so think of every possible angle to announce the appearance of the personality in advance to draw a crowd of potential customers.

[ ] This idea or its modification could work for my business.

#85 Special Events

Special events can be staged to generate excitement and publicity for a company or an organization. Here are four examples. Every year in the Spring, a local restaurant called the Marble Club holds an annual marble shooting contest with the proceeds going to charity. The staff of one hospital challenged another to a hospital bed pushing race down the city's main street. A landscaping company built a large sand castle on its grounds. A bicycle shop held a bike repair clinic. Special events can include open houses, tours, late-night sales and holiday activities. When planning a special event, be sure to notify the news media to try and obtain some publicity. Remember, special events should be designed to increase awareness and attract new customers, as well as generate some excitement and interest in the event. Be sure to plan a special event well in advance and try to anticipate all the details that must be executed to make the event a success. Always advertise and promote the event in order to get participation; otherwise, you may throw the party and have nobody attend.

[ ] This idea or its modification could work for my business.

#86 Sponsorships

Carefully selected business sponsorships can create attention, help establish credibility in the community and reach a target market at a reasonable cost. Sponsorships can even produce sales if, for example, your sponsorship of an event is tied into having the organizers purchase and sell your product at the event. By visibly supporting your target market's favorite activities or charities you enhance the image of your company while reinforcing your message through life-style identification. Some sponsorships also can provide an entertainment event for you to host your preferred customers and an opportunity to sample, display or demonstrate your products. Sponsorship of a Little League team, bowling team, tennis tournament, charitable event, turtle race, or a marble shoot can create attention and raise public awareness about your business. However, unless carefully designed to do so, don't expect these sponsorships to produce immediate sales. Sponsorships do provide goodwill, raise awareness and help to solidify the loyalty of existing customers. That is why established businesses most frequently use sponsorships as part of their overall public relations effort. If you chose to do sponsorships, make sure they relate in some way to your business and look to the long term for results.

[ ] This idea or its modification could work for my business.

#87 Thank You Letters

Always find a way to thank your customers and clients. Send a thank you letter or postcard to all clients and customers who make major purchases. Personalize the thank you as much as possible and indicate how pleased you would be if the recent customer would make referrals to your company. This tool is simple, easy and effective. Yet, it is surprising how many business owners never take the time to show appreciation to their customers and clients. Also, be sure to thank referral sources for sending you business. A major bank lost a valuable customer who had referred thousands upon thousands of dollars of business to the bank, as well as personally controlled several accounts with huge deposits. The banker never bothered to acknowledge the source of the referrals, let alone send a verbal or written thank you. As a result, the referral source felt unappreciated and moved his business and his referrals elsewhere. His comment tells the whole story when he said, "I guess you just have to move your business around to keep from being taken for granted."

[ ] This idea or its modification could work for my business.

#88 Tours

Offer tours of your manufacturing plant, store or business to potential customers or clients to show them how you manage the business. These tours also can be used successfully to generate goodwill by including them with an open house in which you invite the families of employees and perhaps residents in the neighborhood. Add some light refreshments and the tour can go a long way toward creating understanding and appreciation for your business. Try to include a demonstration if appropriate and hand out literature that provides additional information about the company.

[ ] This idea or its modification could work for my business.

CHAPTER FIVE

SALES INCENTIVES

Sales incentives are methods used to get the prospective customers to try your goods or services. Sales incentives of one kind or another have been used effectively by most companies. Some companies depend on them heavily to promote their business. For most businesses, sales incentives should be only a part of a total promotion plan. In addition, they should be carefully selected and planned so they reach and motivate primarily new, preferred customers. Unfortunately, many sales incentive programs are wasted on loyal customers who are already willing to pay full price for the product and who do not require an incentive to purchase again. Of all the methods available to promote a business, sales incentive methods can be the most risky and the most costly.

Sales incentives remain attractive because they can have a dramatic, instant effect on sales. They are designed to entice the potential customer or client to try an offering for the first time or buy more than planned. Before you jump on the sales incentive bandwagon, remember marketing experts have long agreed that all good incentives must do four things to be successful.

First, they should support and enhance the image of the business. The sales incentive should be appropriate for the business and should be able to help improve the company's position in the market place.

Second, they should inspire the user to purchase the product again. Just getting a customer to try a product once is not enough. Incentives should be designed to encourage repeat sales.

Third, they should be aimed at prospects and should motivate them to buy. Many sales incentive programs fail because they do not reach or motivate potential new customers.

Finally, they should create some sense of urgency. Prospects should feel that if they don't act now, they will lose an important opportunity.

Sales incentives have some real pitfalls that must be considered before a business owner decides to include them in the company's promotion plan.

Unfortunately, all sales incentives only provide short-term gains. Stop the incentives, and you usually stop the sales. Incentives can give an immediate boost to the bottom line, but usually will not sustain growth once the incentive is withdrawn. In addition, people who are enticed by sales incentives are not inclined to become loyal customers. Unfortunately, if enticed to buy through a sales incentive, most of these customers often will not return to buy at the regular price. They will require another sales incentive to purchase again. Finally, all sales incentives have a big impact on profit - they reduce it. All sales incentives have a direct or indirect price cutting or profit eroding effect. Therefore, a sales incentive program must make up in volume what it will lose in profit margins. Nevertheless, in most highly competitive businesses, it is not possible to completely avoid sales incentive programs and still survive.

#89 Contests

Contests and games can attract customers and appeal to everyone's desire to be the lucky winner. You should be careful to check with your lawyer to be sure a proposed contest or sweepstakes is legal in your area. Cash is the most attractive prize, but other items will do nicely. You might consider offering your products as the prize. One art supply store held a children's coloring contest by offering free, blank posters at the checkout counter. Parents made additional purchases of crayons, magic markers and colored pencils to give their children a better chance to win. To enter, the completed poster had to be returned to the store. This created another buying opportunity. The prize? Art supplies, naturally. And, since the promotional expenses were shared by three stores in the chain, the cost was minuscule. Offering your product as a prize can help you develop a mailing list of prospects interested in your offerings from those participating in the contest. Also, you may wish to offer a consolation prize to contestants who do not win. A small, inexpensive item can be offered, if the contest loser is willing to come to your place of business to pick it up. Once in the store, the loser may be enticed to buy your goods and services. Remember, games and contests should be fun and exciting. The more you can involve the customer in the contest, the better.

[ ] This idea or its modification could work for my business.

#90 Discount Coupons

The discount coupon is a commonplace and popular method to get people to try products or services for the first time. They can be attached to the product for immediate redemption, handed out with canvassing, given with free samples, mailed separately or with other material. You may wish to distribute special coupons to separate target market groups. Coupons can be distributed in hundreds of ways, so print thousands. Hand out coupons at trade fairs, swap coupons with another company to use as package stuffers, pin coupons on community bulletin boards, put them on car windshields in parking lots, send them along with your billings. Be sure to put the name and location of your company or store on the coupon, as well as information about the product and discount. Put a time limit on the coupon to create a sense of urgency. Studies show that only about three percent of the coupons distributed are ever redeemed. Moreover, a coupon must offer at least a 20 percent discount to be effective. Try to put your coupons in the hands of non-customers. Unfortunately, about 60 percent of the coupons redeemed are done so by loyal consumers who would have gladly paid full price. Therefore, be sure to target your coupons to prospects, not existing customers.

[ ] This idea or its modification could work for my business.

#91 Discount Premium Books

If you have products or services in the food or entertainment industry, consider placing an ad in local discount premium books. They generally contain coupons making two-for-one offers or discounts that are redeemed at the business. You can easily test to see how much new business was brought in through this method by simply saving the coupons and checking the results. Have customers who redeem the coupons write their name and address on the back. Use the information to develop a mailing list and send them advertising and sales information. Just because customers tried your establishment once by using the premium book coupon doesn't mean they will remember to visit your business again. It takes several visits to get a customer into the habit of selecting your business and thinking of you first.

[ ] This idea or its modification could work for my business.

#92 Free Trials

If your product or service lends itself to a "free" trial offer, consider this incentive for your potential customers. Free trial offers should not be limited to test driving cars or a visit to the health spa. One accountant offers the first hour of consultation free to prospective clients. Some appliance companies offer a 30-day, free home trial period for qualified customers. The whole idea behind free trial offers is simple. If you try it, you will like it, and if you like it, you will buy it. Free trial offers are especially suited for items that do not attain immediate customer acceptance or items and services that people are reluctant to purchase for fear that they will not like it once they have bought it.

[ ] This idea or its modification could work for my business.

#93 Gifts & Premiums

For businesses with big ticket items or services, offering a free gift or premium with the purchase can be an incentive to get the customer to buy. Try to tie-in the promotion with another company to stretch the effectiveness of the incentive and lower the cost of the gifts and premiums. Even vendors with smaller ticket items or services might consider this approach. Offer an item free or at a greatly reduced cost with a minimum purchase of your product. "Buy $20.00 or more of any of our products and receive a free set of four holiday goblets." "Open your account with us and receive a free pocket calculator." If you decide to use gifts or premiums, make sure the items you choose are attractive to and appropriate for your potential customers. A good example is a dog food company that once offered a dog obedience training book free with the purchase of a fifty-pound sack of dog food.

[ ] This idea or its modification could work for my business.

#94 Multiple Purchase Offers

When you offer a customer "one free" good or service after they have purchased a certain number, you are making a multiple purchase offer. Donut shops, hair cutting salons, ice cream parlors and car washes have used this successfully to get customers to keep coming back. Once a customer has made 5 or 10 purchases, the next one is free. To keep track of the purchases, issue each customer a small card they can keep in their wallet and punch a hole in the card with each purchase. Or, you can keep the customer cards on file at your business and record the purchases yourself. Multiple purchase offers usually get the customer back several times. Rarely, however, do most customers complete the number of purchases required to get the "one free."

[ ] This idea or its modification could work for my business.

#95 Price Specials

Family rates, student and senior discounts, and group discounts are just some of the ways you can offer price incentives to attract a certain segment of the market. Don't use this tactic on groups that are already willing to pay full price. This incentive should be offered to new markets you wish to attract. Seniors are especially attracted to businesses who offer special treatment for senior citizens. Since they usually have lots of time, seniors are more willing to go out of their way to do business at an establishment that is perceived to give them a special price. Family rates appeal to larger families that must make their dollars stretch. One motel chain offered a family rate by allowing the kids to sleep for free in the room with their parents. They even provided extra roll-away beds, if necessary.

[ ] This idea or its modification could work for my business.

#96 Rebates

Offering a cash rebate for a purchase of a product can stimulate sales. If the purchaser must complete a form and provide proof of purchase to obtain the rebate, it is surprising how many won't bother. This is often the case, even when the offer of the rebate was the incentive to make the purchase in the first place. Small ticket items can offer rebates of $1 - $5, and be just as successful in moving goods as the car manufacturer who offers rebates of $500 or more. The consumer finds rebates less desirable than other price incentives because he has to work harder to get the savings.

[ ] This idea or its modification could work for my business.

#97 Referral Incentives

Offer an incentive for referrals. Money is very attractive and some businesses offer finder's fees to individuals that make successful referrals. Gifts, prizes and merchandise also can be offered as an incentive to get current customers and associates to refer business to your company. Regardless of how large or small the referral incentive is, always be sure to thank the referral source. The thank-you is often more important to the referring party than the reward. Some businesses announce the referral programs up front to the potential referral source and encourage them to participate. Others find it more tasteful to simply acknowledge a referral with a flower arrangement, gift certificate to a restaurant or small gift immediately after the unsolicited referral has been made. All referral incentives should be in keeping with industry practices and the company image. Referral incentives can be very effective when it comes to getting other people to send you customers.

[ ] This idea or its modification could work for my business.

81

#98 Sampling

Hand out free samples of your product or give away a sampling of your service to potential customers. Hire someone in an unusual costume to draw attention to the give away item. Hand out samples on busy street corners or at public entrances to shopping malls. If practical, place the sample in a plastic bag and deliver door-to-door, hanging samples on door knobs. Samples can be mailed or included with another product or service. Be sure to give information about where to obtain the product at the time of sampling. It also is a good time to hand out a discount coupon as an additional incentive to get the potential consumer to buy the product, after he has tried the sample. Sampling also can work for services. For example, a laundromat may give away two plastic coins that can be redeemed for a free wash and dry. An accountant might give away the first hour of service free. Also, consider giving your service away "free" to those who can be strong referral sources for your business. Having referral sources sample your abilities first-hand will give them greater confidence in making referrals to your business.

[ ] This idea or its modification could work for my business.

#99 Special Sales

Don't just have a sale, have a happening. Some stores have "midnight madness sales" and open their doors at midnight to clear out old inventory or special purchases. One store had a "crack of dawn sale" and offered free breakfast in the parking lot for everyone who made a purchase of $25 or more. A sidewalk sale also is an old standby. The idea is to do something so unusual that your company will be remembered for its special sale event.

[ ] This idea or its modification could work for my business.

#100 Tie-ins with Other Products.

Identify other products and services that are used by the same target market as your business. Look for inventive ways to jointly promote your products. For example, offer your product or service as a prize to a radio or TV show for use in return for a negotiated number of mentions about your product. Have your brochure distributed in another company's packaging. A pizza company offered free soft drinks with a purchase, while the soft drink company gave pizza coupons with its product. Have your coupon or flier inserted in the billing statements of other companies. Have small samples of your product and a coupon inserted in the box or package of another product. Then, have the other company announce the sample insert on its packaging as an incentive to get people to buy its product. Both companies will benefit from these arrangements. With some imagination, compatible service companies also can implement successful tie-in promotions.

[ ] This idea or its modification could work for my business.

#101 Two-for-One Offers

Offering two-for-the-price-of-one can be an effective method to get two people to try your product for the first time. Twofers, as they are called by marketing professionals, work well for events charging admission, but also have been successful with goods and services. Limit the offering to a short time period to create some urgency. Two-for-one offers are better than offering 50 percent off because they either move two items with each purchase or introduce two customers to the product or service.

[ ] This idea or its modification could work for my business.

CHAPTER SIX

Organizing Your Activities

Now that you have discovered 101 Big Ideas for promoting your business, go back through the handbook and review the activities you checked. Think again about your target market and your prospective customers. Carefully consider whether or not the methods you checked will be effective ways to reach and motivate your prospects.

Next, determine if your budget can afford to implement the activities you have selected. Remember, you must repeat the activity several times to get the prospective customer's attention. So, determine if your budget can afford to repeat the method often enough during the next year to be effective. Then, select the best 10-12 methods you think will work for your business and list them on the following page.

PROMOTIONAL METHODS

1._____

2._____

3._____

4._____

5._____

6._____

7._____

8._____

9._____

10._____

11._____

12._____

Key Sales Messages

Now, list the advantages of your offering and the reasons why your goods or services should appeal to potential customers. List the benefits, both practical and psychological, that your product offers. Your messages may have to do with convenience, price, quality, or friendly service. To get consumer attention, use words and phrases like "save," "brand new," "results proven," "easy," "free," "effective," "now," "guarantee" and "sale" in your key sales messages. These messages should be incorporated into all your promotional activities, including advertising, packaging, personal sales, public relations/publicity and sales incentives.

LIST THE KEY SALES MESSAGES OF YOUR PRODUCT(S):

_____

_____

_____

_____

_____

_____

_____

_____

Develop a Sales Slogan

Review both the information on sales slogans found on page 7 and your key sales messages. In ten words or less, describe your company's greatest asset in the eyes of your customers. Use this as your sales slogan.

Sales Slogan:

Now, consider if your sales slogan and key sales messages can be effectively delivered through the promotion methods you are considering. Make any necessary adjustments to the activities you selected and listed on page 87, and write the best 10-12 methods on the chart on page 93. Determine the frequency of use and the annual estimated cost of each activity. Add any helpful comments in the space provided. When you are finished, you will have an easy-to-follow promotion plan for your business. Review the plan each month to determine what specific activities you should be implementing. The following promotion plans are examples of ones for a flower shop and a business consulting firm and should provide a better idea of what your promotion plan chart should look like.

Promotion Plan Flower Warehouse

Promotional Method	Frequency	Annual Cost	Comments
Yellow Pages	Daily	$2,400	Monitor Results
Window Signs	12 x Year	$360	Support Promotions
Point of Purchase Signs	12 x Year	$240	Support Promotions
Newspaper Ads	2 x Month	$3,000	Support Promotions
Fliers	12 x Year	$800	With Sales Promotions
Sales Promotions	1 x Month	$4,500	Holidays & Specials
Publicity	12 x Year	$200	Publicize Promotions
Personal Sales Calls	1 x Week	$0	Corporate Accounts
Sampling & Gifts	as needed	$1,000	Door Prizes Referrals
Networking	1 x Week	$600	Sales Leads
Thank You Letters	as needed	$0	Customers Referrals

Promotion Plan - Sure Success Consultants

Promotional Method	Frequency	Annual Cost	Comments
Yellow Pages	Daily	$720	
Classified Display Ad	Weekly	$1020	Local Bus. Newspaper
Newsletter	Quarterly	$600	Clients & Prospects
Brochure	Daily	$750	All-purpose Sales Tool
Public Speaking	2xMonth	$0	Mostly Time
Networking	1xWeek	$600	Leads Club
Letters & Proposals	4xWeek	$100	To Prospects Personalize
Publicity	2xYear	$100	2 Campaigns
Free Seminars	4xYear	$800	Generate Leads
Display	1xYear	$600	Bus. Fair
Folders	Weekly	$350	For Impact
Postcards	Monthly	$1,200	Announce Services

Promotion Plan - Your Company

Promotional Method	Frequency	Annual Cost	Comments

Important Reminders

If you fail to let potential customers or clients know about the benefits they will receive from your goods or services, or if you do little or nothing to promote your business, it is unlikely that your business will be able to survive or prosper. Promoting your business stimulates sales and sales make your business a success.

You will feel more comfortable promoting your business with a simple, carefully crafted plan of action in which you select 10-12 promotional activities that will reach and motivate your potential customers. Use information you gather from your current customer base to help you determine the best methods. Talking to your customers is the easiest and most affordable means of doing market research. Your customers will probably come up with your sales slogan, if you simply ask them what they like best about your business. In addition, they can tell you about how they learned about your business in the first place and which promotional methods they respond to most frequently. Once you have selected the appropriate activities, you must make a strong commitment to your plan and implement it on a consistent basis.

Your plan will fail if you do not set aside time, energy and money to put the plan into action.

Make sure that the messages you deliver to your prospects will motivate them to buy from you. The messages you send are as important to the success of your promotion plan as the methods you use as vehicles to send them. Again, rely on your current customers to help you select the most effective messages. Understand what your customers need and want from you and stress how your business can satisfy those needs better than your competitors. From your customer's point of view, describe your greatest business asset or the most appealing aspect of your business in ten words or less and turn it into your sales slogan. Remember, repeat your sales slogan in all your advertising and promotional activities.

Stick to your plan. Don't panic if you don't get instant results. Few promotional plans that are implemented on a small budget ever become an overnight success. You must be willing to give your plan time to work. Again, you can increase the effectiveness of your promotional activities by consistently repeating them as often as your budget can afford. It is better to do a few things well and repeat them over and over, than it is to do many things once or once in awhile. Evaluate the effectiveness of each of your promotional activities only after you have given each one enough time to fairly judge the results. For example, a newsletter must be mailed at least quarterly and for at least one year before a business owner should judge the effectiveness of this method. On the other hand, a local newspaper campaign may only require a three-month trial to determine its worth - again, only if you run the ad often enough for people to see it.

Try to have fun promoting your business. That will help get rid of some of the anxiety business owners often feel about marketing, advertising and promotion and about spending money on these activities. Most business owners would love to just manufacture the goods or provide the service without having to go out and attract customers. They wish the orders would just come in the door or the mailbox without any marketing effort. Unfortunately, that rarely happens. So, if your business survival must depend on promoting your goods and services, you might as well try and have some fun doing it.

Many promotional activities allow the business owner to personally get to know their customers. Often they discover they really enjoy the company of their customers and have things in common with them other than the business relationship. Friendships develop. Some promotional activities also offer an opportunity to entertain clients, support interests outside the business or make a contribution to the community. When this happens, you should view the activity not only as an investment in the company's promotion plan, but also as one of the side benefits of business ownership.

I wish I could credit the marketing genius who came up with the saying "people just love to buy from people who love to sell." That person was right on the money. There is nothing as effective as enthusiasm when it comes to promoting your business, selling your goods/services or convincing another business owner to do a joint promotion with you. Enthusiasm is contagious, it's also a powerful tool of persuasion. So, be enthusiastic about your business and about promoting it every chance you get.

Finally, of all the activities a business owner must undertake to develop and manage a successful business, promotional activities - advertising, packaging, personal sales, public relations/publicity and sales incentives - conducted on behalf of the company have the most impact when it comes to telling the world about what kind of business the owner operates. A company's promotional activities are the windows through which an outsider first sees into a business and often they determine whether or not the outsider will open the door and step in.

ORDERTODAY!

101 BIG IDEAS FOR
PROMOTING A BUSINESS
ON A SMALL BUDGET

Makes a great gift for a business associate or someone just starting a new business.   Give a copy to a friend or provide a copy to all your small business customers. Quantity discounts are available. This book is so valuable, no small business owner should be without one. Simply use the handy form below to order extra copies.

101 BIG IDEAS FOR PROMOTING A BUSINESS ON A SMALL BUDGET is Great! Send me _____ copy(s). I've enclosed $11.50 for each book and postage/handling or authorized the use of my credit card for payment.

Name _____

Business _____

Address_____

City_____State_____   Zip_____

Signature_____

[ ] VISA #   _____
[ ] MasterCard #   _____
Expiration Date   _____

Send to: **Marketing Methods Press**
                  1413 E. Marshall Avenue
                  Phoenix, AZ 85014
                  (602) 840-7308
Please make checks payable to Marketing Methods. Allow 4-6 weeks for delivery.

"For several years we have been working to develop a good collection of resources for the small business owner, and we are very pleased to have this excellent addition to that collection. This is a popular area and I know that the book will get a lot of use."

Karen Drake
Library Manager, City of Chandler Public Library

"*101 Big Ideas...* simplifies the process with a straightforward, simple approach to marketing without using textbook language or complicated jargon. It's full of examples..."

Business Opportunities Journal

"With apologies to Mao Tse-tung, Barbara Lambesis has come up with a little red book to help small business owners promote their businesses. Entitled *101 Big Ideas for Promoting a Business on a Small Budget*, the slim volume provides practical suggestions on how entrepreneurs can promote their firm without spending a lot of time and money."

The Toledo Blade

"The book is chock-full of ideas ranging from take one racks and door hangers to balloons, gifts, premiums and newsletters, plus 94 blockbuster ideas for a small budget."

Small Business Opportunities

"*101 Big Ideas for Promoting a Business on a Small Budget* is a guide for owners to follow and promote their business."

The Flagstaff Sun

"Importantly, the book doesn't just make suggestions, it tells how to implement them."

The St. Louis Countain

"I purchased your book and am finding it fun and easy to read and chock-full of possibilities!"

Jan Briski
Coldwell Banker Residential Real Estate

"*101 Big Ideas for Promoting a Business on a Small Budget* offers readers a simple, straightforward approach to developing a do-it-yourself promotion plan. The book takes the mystery out of marketing and provides the reader with low cost ideas they can put into action immediately."

Cottage Connection
Newsletter of the National Association for the Cottage Industry

"Rest assured, after reading this book, you'll have new ideas you can apply to your own situation."

Perspectives

"Lambesis provides [Big Ideas] 101 of them in an easy-to-read format that provides working pages at the end for developing an individual marketing plan. Her idea is to take the mystery and fear out of marketing for business owners who, because of budget constraints, can't hire someone to develop expensive marketing campaigns."

Arizona Republic

"Ideas in the book are easy to understand and simple to implement. The authors do an excellent job of taking the mystery out of marketing and providing readers with low cost ideas that can be put into action immediately."

Purchasing Management, Canada